Influential Latinos

PABLO NERUDA

Nobel Prize-Winning Poet

Jeanne Nagle and Jodie A. Shull

Enslow Publishing
101 W. 23rd Street
Suite 240
New York, NY 10011
USA
enslow.com

For Russell, Poet and Painter — Jodie A. Shull

Acknowledgments: With thanks to Edith, Judith, Donna, Karen, Connie, Suzan, Stephanie, Marie, and Nina— teachers and women of wisdom! —Jodie A. Shull

Published in 2016 by Enslow Publishing, LLC
101 W. 23rd Street, Suite 240, New York, NY 10011

Library of Congress Cataloging-in-Publication Data
Nagle, Jeanne.
 Pablo Neruda : Nobel Prize-winning poet / Jeanne Nagle and Jodie A. Shull.
   pages cm. — (Influential Latinos)
 Includes bibliographical references and index.
 Summary: "Describes the life and accomplishments of Chilean poet Pablo Neruda"— Provided by publisher.
 ISBN 978-0-7660-7314-2
 1. Neruda, Pablo, 1904-1973—Juvenile literature. 2. Poets, Chilean—20th century—Biography—Juvenile
literature. I. Shull, Jodie A. II. Title.
 PQ8097.N4Z71954 2016
 861'.62—dc23
 [B]
                              2015029186

Printed in the United States of America

To Our Readers: We have done our best to make sure all website addresses in this book were active and appropriate when we went to press. However, the author and the publisher have no control over and assume no liability for the material available on those websites or on any websites they may link to. Any comments or suggestions can be sent by e-mail to customerservice@enslow.com.

Portions of this book originally appeared in *Pablo Neruda Passion, Poetry, and Politics*, by Jodie A. Shull.

Photo Credits: Cover, p. 1 Angelo Cozzi/Mondadori Portfolio/Getty Images; p. 4 Jean-Regis Rouston/Roger Viollet/Getty Images; p. 7, 61, 100, Associated Press; p. 9 Nat Farbman/The LIFE Picture Collection/Getty Images; p. 13 The Print Collector/Hulton Archive/Getty Images; p. 15 Photo12/Universal Images Group/Getty Images; p. 17 Hulton Archive/Getty Images; p. 19 Leo Rosenthal/Pix Inc./The LIFE Images Collection/Getty Images; p. 27 Santi Visalli/Archive Photos/Getty Images; 31 Superstock; p. 35 Roger Viollet Collection/Getty Images; p. 37 E. O. Hoppe/Getty Images; p. 37 E. O. Hoppe/Hulton Archive/Getty Images; pp. 56 Album/Oronoz/Album/Superstock; p. 43 Universal History Archive/Universal Images Group/Getty Images; p. 46 Mondadori Portfolio/Getty Images; p. 49 ullstein bild/Getty Images; p. 53 ullstein bild/Getty Images; p. 59 Martin Bernetti/AFP/Getty Images; p. 63 IML/Superstock; p. 69 Eliot Elisofon/The LIFE Picture Collection/Getty Images; p. 72 Paul Popper/Popperfoto/Getty Images; p. 76 RIA Novosti/Alamy; p. 80 © AGIP / Bridgeman Images; p. 83 Michael Mauney/The LIFE Images Collection/Getty Images; p. 87 Keystone/Hulton Archive/Getty Images; p. 90 GDA via AP Images; p. 94 Hulton Archive/Getty Images; p. 96 Keystone-France/Gamma-Keystone/Getty Images; p. 100 STF/AFP/Getty Images; p. 106 Marcelo Montecino/Moment/Getty Images; p. 108 FP/Getty Images; p. 110 © Maxime Dube/Alamy Stock Photo.

Excerpts from *MEMOIRS* by Pablo Neruda, translated by Hardie St. Martin. Translation copyright © 1977 by Farrar, Straus and Giroux, LLC.

Contents

Pablo Neruda was a Chilean Nobel Prize-winning poet and diplomat. He is often considered the twentieth century's greatest poet.

Chapter 1

A MAN OF GREAT RESOURCES

The great Spanish painter Pablo Picasso had been keeping a secret for weeks, and the moment of revelation was almost at hand. Events were winding down at the 1949 meeting of the World Congress of the Partisans of Peace as Picasso anxiously scanned the crowd, looking for a certain familiar face. At last, he spied the special guest he had arranged to have speak before the gathered writers, artists, scientists, and scholars.

The two friends greeted each other, then Picasso and his surprise guest listened as the conference chairman stepped up to the podium. He told the crowd that the special guest had only been in the hall for a few short minutes, "for he is a hunted man. . . . He is Pablo Neruda."[1]

The World Peace Council

The World Congress of the Partisans of Peace was the second meeting of an organization that has become known as the World Peace Council. The organization was formed to seek international cooperation among nations to achieve lasting peace in the world. This meeting of artists, writers, musicians, scientists, and other intellectuals from around the world had significant ties to the Communist Party and the teachings of Vladimir Lenin.[2] Early council members believed that Communism was the only form of government that could lead the world toward peace and unity.

Early goals of the Council were the abolishment of nuclear weapons and stopping participation in what the council deemed unjust wars. Although it was supposed to be an international effort, members of the Council often spoke out against the "aggressive" United States.

The World Peace Council still exists. However, since the fall of the former Soviet Union, the organization has become a much less significant player in efforts toward world peace.

Silence fell over the hall. Then delegates from nearly every continent rose to their feet with a thundering cheer. Pablo Neruda was alive!

A Year Away

Indeed, Neruda stood before the conference delegates in good health and good spirits. No official news of Neruda, the renowned poet and statesman of Chile, had been heard for more than a year. Friends and colleagues around the globe feared that Neruda had been put in prison by the government of Chile. The government had taken away many of the people's freedoms. People like Neruda, who spoke out in protest, had been arrested and were never heard from again. They simply disappeared.

Fortunately, Neruda was a man of great resources. The fugitive Neruda had an international brotherhood

Pablo Picasso kisses Pablo Neruda after introducing the poet to the audience at the 1949 World Congress of the Partisans of Peace.

of poets and friends who helped him flee to safety.[3] His many friends and admirers in Chile had hidden the beloved poet from the government police. After many months, they managed to smuggle him over the Andes Mountains into Argentina, then across the ocean to Europe. Once he arrived in Paris, friends such as Picasso had helped him secure a valid passport and the legal right to stay in France.

Worldwide Solidarity

Neruda was thrilled that his time in hiding had at last come to an end. Adding to his relief and joy was the fact that, at that moment in Paris, he was among people who were as dedicated to the causes of peace and tolerance as he was. Smiling and waving at the crowd, Neruda began his first public speech in more than a year:

> Dear friends . . . if I have arrived a bit late at your meeting, it is due to the difficulties I have had to overcome in order to get here. I bring you the greetings of all the people in distant lands. The political persecution which exists in my country has allowed me to appreciate the fact that human solidarity is greater than all barriers."[4]

Neruda also read a poem from his new book, published secretly in Chile. This early edition of *Canto General* (*General Song*), written over the previous ten years, was Neruda's tribute to the Americas. He hoped his *Canto General* would describe and celebrate the history, the land, the life, and the struggles of all the people of the Americas.[5] For Neruda, the struggle for

His shocking appearance in Paris was the start of Neruda's popularity in Europe and North America.

peace and justice in the Americas mirrored the same cause for people in all nations. The love and respect for life that rang through Neruda's poetry had made him a champion of human rights to all who knew his work.

The Poet's Voice

Neurda's arrival in Paris began a new chapter in the poet's life. Already known and loved throughout Latin America, Neruda's poetry would soon reach readers throughout Europe and in English-speaking North America as well.[6] In Paris that year and during his later world travels, he would find new friends and new experiences to enrich his poetry. Like his good friend Picasso, Neruda always had a new creative dream to follow. He never stopped learning and growing in his chosen art.

From his youth in the cold rain forests of southern Chile through years of diplomatic work, travel, and political action, Pablo Neruda wrote poetry. In his vast outpouring of poems, the story of his life unfolds. He said, "If you ask me what my poetry is, I must say, I don't know; but if you ask my poetry, it will tell you who I am!"[7] He hoped to speak to and for all people. Readers have responded to his voice with fascination and love from the very beginning.

Chapter 2

NATURE BOY

The story of Pablo Neruda began in Parral, a small town in central Chile, on July 12, 1904. His given name was Ricardo Eliecer Neftalí Reyes Basoalto,[1] but the family simply called him Neftalí. His mother, Rosa, contracted tuberculosis and died when Nefaltí was just a month old. The infant lived with his grandparents on their farm in Parral while his railroad-conductor father, José del Carmen, worked.

When Neftalí was two years old, his father remarried. The boy's stepmother, Doña Trinidad Candia Marverde, took extra-good care of him, nursing the sickly youngster through a number of illnesses. By the time Neftalí entered school at age six, Doña Trinidad had taught him to read and write. He later called his stepmother "the guardian angel of my childhood."[2]

The Move to Temuco

Don José, had resettled the family in the village of Temuco, on the edge of the rain forests of southern Chile.

In 1906, Temuco was a frontier town of rough wooden houses and muddy streets. Settlers from many different countries shared the region with the Mapuche Indians.

The weather in Temuco was as dramatic as the rain forests and mountains—many of which were volcanoes—that surrounded the town. The summers were hot, and the town's roads were filled with dust. In the winter, they were thick with mud. The rain, which Neftalí would later call an "unforgettable presence,"[3] sometimes caused rivers to flood, washing away houses along the banks. From his bedroom window, Neftalí would watch as the wild wind blew through the trees, sometimes lifting the roof from a neighboring house. "Each house was a ship struggling to make port in the ocean of winter," he later wrote.[4] The area was also prone to frequent earthquakes, causing the town to tremble.

A Unique Location

West of the Andes Mountains in northern Chile is a cool, wet region known as a temperate rain forest. Like the tropical rain forests near the Equator, these cool forests are home to a rich variety of plants and animals. Many of the trees, birds, and mammals that call Chile's rain forests home are found nowhere else on Earth. These include the world's smallest deer and one of the world's largest woodpeckers. This forest is also home to the huge araucaria, or "monkey puzzle," tree, with its dense tangle of branches. The araucaria is the world's oldest type of tree, first appearing on Earth about 200 million years ago.

Little Things Mean a Lot

Early on, Neftalí had developed a deep curiosity about the natural world. He was fascinated with the rich plant and animal life that called the rain forest home. He spent his free time exploring, collecting bird's nests and eggs, spiders, beetles, leaves, ferns, pinecones—whatever small treasures he could find. A friend recalled that, he had an unquenchable curiosity for strange stones, pieces of wood and insects that he never lost.[5]

Neftalí also loved the solitary activities of reading and writing. His aunts said that he might look weak but he had a will of iron.[6] A school friend described Neftalí

Neruda came from a rough frontier town in Chile. His connection to the natural world made its way into his poetry.

as very thin, and very serious, with an absentminded expression, arriving late for classes."[7] Another friend, who joined him in exploring the countryside "looking at the world's little things," said Neftalí had a special quality, "a style that belonged only to him and made him different."[8]

He was never much interested in the sports and games the other boys played. Neftalí always lost the acorn fights they had. He enjoyed watching the acorns fly through the air so much that he forgot to dodge the ones that rained down on him. "While I was busy examining the marvelous acorn, green and polished, with its gray wrinkled hood . . . a downpour of acorns would pelt my head," he wrote.[9]

The Birth of a Poet

Neftalí's father worked as the conductor of a train that carried sand and rocks. The region's heavy rain washed away the soil that held up the railroad tracks. Crews of men worked constantly to build up the land under the tracks. His father sometimes took Neftalí out of school and brought him along on overnight train trips. On these trips, while the workers collected the materials they needed, Neftalí was free to explore the forest. His father—a stern, hardworking man—hoped to interest his son in the practical world and lure him away from his constant reading and writing.

By age ten, Neftalí knew he wanted to be a poet, something his father would never approve. "I was not yet writing verse," he later wrote, "but I was already a poet."[10] His love of nature and the wonder he felt in the forest inspired him to write. He described himself as a distant, reserved solitary observer who clung to the wall like moss.[11]

Neftalí spent his evenings writing in his school notebooks and reading whatever books he could find. Novels by Russian authors Tolstoy and Dostoyevsky, poetry by Frenchmen Rimbaud and Baudelaire, adventure stories by Jules Verne, and the Spanish classic *Don Quixote* were some of his favorites. Through books, he traveled the world and discovered its wonders. He

Neruda's father was a train conductor. He hoped to interest his dreamy son in a practical profession.

.later recalled, "The sack of human wisdom had broken open. . . . Reading, I didn't sleep or eat."[12]

Waves and Books

One hot summer, Neftalí's family went to spend a month with friends living near the ocean. The family packed most of their household goods for the trip, including the mattresses to sleep on. Neftalí, his older stepbrother, Rodolfo, and his younger half-sister, Laura, set out with their parents for the journey to the sea. They traveled west by train and riverboat to the coastal town of Puerto Saavedra, where they could hear the ocean waves pounding. Neftalí found himself "overwhelmed" by his first sight of the ocean. The white-capped waves sounded to him like "the loud pounding of a gigantic heart, the heartbeat of the universe."[13] His father insisted that Neftalí and Laura go out in the ocean every day. They were terrified of the rough, icy water and held hands tightly while the waves crashed around them.

During this first visit to the sea, Neftalí learned to ride horses. He enjoyed galloping along the shore. Because he lived in the southern hemisphere, Neftalí's July birthday fell during the bitter Temuco winter. To escape the hot, scorching summers in Temuco, his family made many more trips to the ocean in the summer months of January and February. Exploring the land suited Neftalí well. He later wrote about those times: "Along endless beaches or thicketed hills, a communion was started between my spirit—that is, my poetry—and the loneliest land in the world. This was many years ago, but that communion, that revelation, that pact with the wilderness, is still a part of my life."[14]

At Puerto Saavedra, Neftalí first saw penguins, wild swans, and flocks of pink flamingos in flight.[15]

THEODOR DOSTOYEFFSKY.

As a boy, Neruda was a voracious reader. Among his favorites were the novels of Dostoyevsky.

Another happy memory of summers in Puerto Saavedra was the small public library Neftalí discovered there. Neftalí remembered the librarian as "a small, white-bearded wizard, the poet Don Augusto Winter." Winter was impressed with Neftalí's love of reading and suggested many new books for his enjoyment. "I would settle myself there [in the library]," Neftalí later wrote, "as if sentenced to read in the three summer months all the books written through the long winters of the world."[16] Neftalí described himself as an ostrich who "gobbled up everything. . . . My appetite for reading did not let up day or night."[17]

When Neftalí was fifteen years old, he met the famous Chilean poet Gabriela Mistral, who had come to Temuco as principal of the local girls' school. Neftalí later wrote that, at first, he was scared of this tall, imposing woman who often wore long dresses and a stern expression. Yet when he got to know her he "found her to be very gracious. In her dark face . . . her very white teeth flashed in a full, generous smile that lit up the room."[18] Mistral, who would later become the first South American to win the Nobel Prize for Literature (1945), encouraged Neftalí in his writing and gave him books to read.

Writing for Fun and Quinces

Neftalí's first poem was one written to his "angelic stepmother whose gentle shadow watched over my childhood."[19] He was almost eleven years old at the time of the writing. He tried to show the poem to his parents while they were deep in conversation. His father looked at the poem and said, "Where did you copy that from?"[20] Neftalí had not copied it, but Don José had no patience for his son's love of writing.

Neftalí had better luck with another writing task he attempted around that time. One of the boys at school asked him to write love letters for him. "I don't remember what these letters were like exactly," Neftalí later wrote, "but they may have been my first literary achievement." When the truth came out that Neftalí was writing the love letters, the girl receiving them gave him a quince,

Poet Gabriela Mistral encouraged Neruda's love of reading. Mistral was also an educator, diplomat, and feminist.

which is a type of fruit. He kept writing the letters on his own behalf and kept receiving quinces.[21]

When he was thirteen years old, Neftalí wrote an essay that appeared in the newspaper *La Mañana*. An older cousin of his, Orlando Mason, was the paper's editor and an influential poet in his own right. Mason gave poetry readings and was a champion for social justice, especially in defense of the local native people. In addition to giving Neftalí his start as a published writer, he was an important role model to the young man.

Neftalí's essay encouraged people to follow their desires with enthusiasm and persistence. He was taking his own advice as he pursued his desire to be a poet.

Adopting an Alias

Neftalí began sending his poems to a larger audience in Chile's capital city of Santiago. In late 1918 and early 1919, sixteen of them were published in the Santiago magazine *Corre-Vuela*. His poems were signed "Neftalí Reyes." This upset his father, who increased his efforts to keep Neftalí from writing poetry. One night, an angry José del Carmen stormed into Neftalí's bedroom, tossed his son's notebooks out the window, and burned them on the patio below.[22]

When he was sixteen years old, Neftalí decided to spare his father the knowledge that he was writing poetry. In October 1920, he began using the pen name "Pablo Neruda" to sign his poems. The pen name soon became Neftalí's new identity. Years later, when asked where he got the name Pablo Neruda, he said he chose the name

Neruda from a magazine. He said he did not realize it was the name of a famous Czech writer, Jan Neruda.[23] He never explained his choice of the name Pablo, the Spanish version of Paul.

In March 1921, Neftalí Reyes, the young man who now called himself Pablo Neruda, left his childhood home in Temuco. His father had agreed to support him as a student at the Pedagogical Institute in the capital city, Santiago. Neftalí agreed to study French and become a language teacher. In José del Carmen's eyes, teaching was a respectable career, unlike writing poetry for a living.

At age sixteen, Pablo Neruda said good-bye to the country landscape he had known and loved and boarded the night train for Santiago and a new life.

Chapter 3

PROTESTS AND PUBLISHING

Attending college in Santiago meant a whole new life for Pablo Neruda. For one thing, the landscape around him had changed dramatically. Gone were the rain forests and other natural wonders Neruda had come to appreciate and love. In their place were the buildings and crowds that populated the capital city. More than his surroundings had changed, however. As a student attending school hundreds of miles from home, Neruda was able to enjoy freedoms that had been denied him while he was living under the watchful, and sometimes disapproving, eye of his father.

He could read and write whenever and for as long as he wanted. He wrote later that he arrived in Santiago with his "head filled with books, dreams, and poems buzzing around like bees."[1]

Moving to the cosmopolitan city of Santiago, Chile's capital, changed Neruda's perspective in several important ways.

Student Poet and Activist

Like most university students, Neruda lived in a boardinghouse. Although he had his small allowance from home, he was poor and often went hungry. He spent his days reading and writing in his room. He finished several poems each day and drank endless cups of tea, which served as a substitute for food when he could not afford to eat.

He said, "I wrote a lot more than I had up until then, but I ate a lot less."[2]

Neruda took to dressing in a black suit, a wide-brimmed black hat, and a long cape that his father had given him. The cape was designed to keep railroad men warm as they worked outside in the harsh winter. For Neruda, it became a symbol of his new life as a poet.[3]

The school year began in March, at the end of summer in Chile. Neruda enrolled at the university to major in French. He soon began spending more time writing poems than studying for his classes. He found a group of friends who shared his love of books and poetry. They spent their evenings together talking far into the night. "Conversations and poems were passed around till daybreak," he later wrote.[4] Times were bad for the average citizen of Chile in the early 1920s. From 1914 to 1918, during World War I, the economy of Chile had thrived. A large market for copper and sodium nitrate, mined from deep within the Atacama Desert in northern Chile, provided jobs for many and created fortunes for wealthy investors. With the end of the war, however, demand for these products fell. Workers were left unemployed and hungry. Many migrated south to Santiago looking for work. They looked to the government for help with job opportunities and fair treatment. In 1918 and 1919, protest rallies and strikes brought violent clashes between workers and government forces.

Students at the university raised their voices in support of the workers. Neruda spent much of his time at the student federation headquarters. Student leaders spoke out for political reform, social justice, a more equal distribution of the country's wealth, and economic opportunity. Student attempts to criticize the government were often met with violence. While still in Temuco, Neruda had learned of a student rebellion that was crushed by the government. Government

Mineral-Rich Barren Land

The Atacama of northern Chile is one of the world's oldest and driest deserts. It averages less than one-half inch (1.3 centimeters) of rain each year. The Atacama is a barren region with almost no plant life, but it contains huge deposits of valuable minerals. The Atacama is rich in copper. It is also the world's only source of natural sodium nitrate, a mineral used for fertilizer and explosives. People have lived in this harsh landscape for about ten thousand years. Because the Atacama is so dry, the artifacts of its ancient people are still in excellent condition. The world's oldest mummies have been found there.

destruction of the student federation headquarters and the killing of a student poet deeply disturbed Neruda.[5]

Working Man

Neruda had published poems in the student magazine *Claridad* even before he arrived in Santiago. As a university student, he began spending his afternoons at the office of the *Claridad*. He published poems and a political column for the magazine. To make a little money, he worked on translations and wrote articles for other magazines and newspapers.

Before long, Neruda lost his small allowance from home when his father found out he was writing poems instead of studying. A little money still came now and then. His stepmother smuggled some to the starving poet through his younger half-sister Laura.

Neruda was a leader among his fellow writers and artists. They admired his poetry as well as his friendly manner and easy laughter. Women liked him very much. He was often seen in the evening walking on the boulevard arm-in-arm with a woman.

Neruda moved from one boardinghouse to another. He sometimes lived with friends and sometimes alone. Neruda was looking for better places to live with little money to pay for them. He carried along his small collection of books and his few clothes.

He spent his days in his room writing. Whenever he had company, Neruda would write, and occasionally look up and speak. It didn't seem to bother him to have someone in the room interrupting his work. Apparently,

The man who would go on to publish many books got his start submitting poems to his university's student journal.

he liked it. It even seemed to help his writing process.[6] During his student days, Neruda discovered the joy of having like-minded friends around him as much as possible.

First Collections

In 1923, when Neruda was nineteen years old, he had a collection of poems ready for his first book. The Chilean student federation published *Crepusculario* (*Twilight Book*). Neruda had to raise the money himself to pay for the printing. He sold a few pieces of furniture, pawned the watch his father had given him, and even parted with his black suit.[7] *Crepusculario*, a name Neruda came up with, contained forty-eight poems, some written when he was still living in Temuco. The poems were filled with themes of sadness, melancholy, and love. Neruda later wrote that he spent many hours watching sunsets and the coming of twilight on the balcony of his boardinghouse in his early student days.[8]

In June 1924, just before his twentieth birthday, Neruda published another book of poetry that would make him famous throughout Latin America. *Viente Poemas de Amor y una Cancíon Desesperada* (*Twenty Love Songs and a Song of Despair*) was immediately popular with readers, who learned many of the verses by heart. These love poems became imprinted in the minds and mouths of Chilean readers, and later the rest of the Spanish-speaking world. And they still are today.[9]

Neruda said the inspiration for these poems came from his love of the natural world of southern Chile and his experiences as a student and writer in the artistic community in Santiago.[10] One friend from that time said that Neruda's two books of poetry quickly made him one of the most famous persons in Chile.[11] Readers loved Neruda's poetry for its heartfelt emotion that they could share. Literary critics admired it, too. Neruda became a celebrity overnight.

Fame, No Fortune

By the age of twenty two, he had published two successful books of poetry, 108 articles in *Claridad*, and many book reviews and literary articles in magazines and newspapers. Unfortunately, Neruda's instant fame did not bring much money. He remained a starving poet. He spent his days reading great works of literature and writing his poetry without much financial reward.

When he went home for summer trips to the beach at Puerto Saavedra with his family, Neruda continued to argue with his father over his writing career. Despite his son's fame, José del Carmen still insisted he was wasting his life trying to be a poet. In fact, Neruda still depended on his stepmother for money to buy food.

Neruda knew his considerable accomplishments could not provide him with a decent living in Chile. When he could, he accepted invitations to visit new places. He visited a friend who was teaching Spanish in Ancud, located on a beautiful island in southern Chile. He also made several visits to the beautiful port city of Valparaíso, on the Pacific coast near Santiago. He wrote, "Santiago is a captive city behind walls of snow.

Valparaíso . . . throws open its doors wide to the infinite sea, to its street cries, to the eyes of children."[12]

Neruda continued to join his friends in Santiago for long evenings of talk and laughter, but they sensed he was longing to leave Chile and travel to other parts of the world.[13] His friends expected a young man with his literary achievements to travel to Europe, specifically to Paris, the world capital of cultural life. Many people asked him why he was in Santiago. Poets like him belonged in Paris.[14]

Poetic Diplomacy

Like many artists and writers in Latin America at the time, Neruda applied for a job representing the government. Providing jobs in the foreign service were a way for the government to support the arts. Work as a foreign consul, or diplomat, carried few responsibilities and left writers time to pursue their literary art. With the help of a wealthy friend, Neruda applied to Chile's foreign minister for work as a diplomat.

He listened as the minister read to him a list of vacant positions overseas. "I managed to catch only one name, which I had never heard or read before: Rangoon."[15] When the Minister asked where he wanted to go, Neruda replied with the only name he could remember, "Rangoon." He had no idea where or what it was. Rangoon was the capital city of Burma, now called Myanmar, a country in Southeast Asia. In fact, when Neruda's friends came to celebrate his new job, he had

Like many Latin American artists, Neruda took a post in the foreign service. He began his career as a diplomat in Rangoon.

forgotten the name of the city and could only tell them that he was bound for Asia.

At a farewell party in Valparaíso, Neruda met an old friend, Alvaro Hinojosa, who made him an attractive offer. If Neruda exchanged his first-class boat ticket for two third-class tickets, his friend could come along, too. Neruda liked Hinojosa. His friend had some experience with foreign travel, which might be very useful since Neruda had none. Neither traveler had much money. Together they boarded the train that would take them over the Andes Mountains to Argentina and on to the Atlantic coast. Their journey to the far side of the earth— and unexpected adventure—had begun.

Chapter 4

BETWEEN WORLDS

On June 18, 1927, just before his twenty-third birthday, Neruda boarded a German steamship bound for Lisbon, Portugal. This ocean voyage marked the second leg of the multipart journey he and his friend, Alvaro Hinojosa, were on as they made their way to Rangoon. Stops in Europe included Spain and France. Instead of meeting some of the French poets he admired during a stopover in Paris, Neruda wound up spending time with a group of Latin American writers, who warmly welcomed him and Hinojosa into their circle. From there they sailed across the Mediterranean Sea to Egypt, where they traveled through the Suez Canal and eventually reached Singapore. The entire trip took four months.

Neruda wrote stories about the trip and sent them home to the Santiago daily newspaper *La Nación*. He still had plenty of time to think about his job as an honorary consul and new living arrangements. He had heard stories during the voyage about the high cost of living in Asia. There were also reports of the many tropical diseases he would face. But what else could he do? He had to submit to the struggles of life.[1]

Welcome to Rangoon

Many adventures awaited Neruda as he learned the ways of diplomacy and the geography of the Far East. Upon arriving in Singapore, he thought he was close to Rangoon, only to discover that his post was miles and miles from the crowded capitol.[2] The Chilean consul in Singapore told Neruda and his friend that they had just missed the boat that could take them to Rangoon. Even worse, there were no funds waiting for them in Singapore. Completely out of money, the two young men had to borrow from the consul to survive the next few days until the boat to Rangoon returned.

At the end of October 1927, they finally reached Rangoon, Burma. In 1927, Burma was part of the British colony of India. Neruda's life in the diplomatic service got off to a very confusing start. He had to find his own housing in an unfamiliar city. His duties as consul from Chile were as small as his salary. "My official duties demanded my attention only once every three months, when a ship arrived . . . bound for Chile with hard paraffin and large cases of tea," he wrote.[3] Once he had stamped and signed papers for the ship, his duties were complete for another three months.

Alone in Burma

Neruda was lonely and restless. He missed the artistic and literary friends who laughed and talked into the night with him in Chile. He missed being surrounded by the musical rhythms of the Spanish language. Since he had little knowledge of spoken English, he felt left out of the social world of the British diplomats around him

In Burma, Neruda found himself unable to communicate. He felt more comfortable with people on the bustling streets.

in Rangoon. Neruda could not speak Burmese either, but he felt more comfortable with the people in the busy streets and marketplaces. Unfortunately, mingling with the Burmese was frowned upon by British society. "These two worlds never touched," he wrote of the British and the Burmese. "The natives were not allowed in the places reserved for the English, and the English lived away from the throbbing pulse of the country."[4]

Feeling depressed and alone, Neruda wrote little poetry during this time. He thought about leaving the diplomatic service and moving to Europe. He complained in a letter to his sister about the terrible heat, both day and night. He said Rangoon was a horrendous exile, and he worried if he went to Europe things would be any better. He complained for feeling poorly and weary.[5] To make matters worse, Alvaro Hinojosa, Neruda's only friend in Burma, had decided to travel on to India.

In April 1928, Neruda's social life momentarily took a turn for the better when he began a love affair with a beautiful Burmese woman who worked in an office in Rangoon. He called her Josie Bliss. Unfortunately, living with a Burmese woman made Neruda even more of an exile from the British community in Rangoon. In time, he grew frightened of Bliss's jealous nature. She said that only if he died would she stop fearing that he would leave her.[6] When Neruda learned that the government of Chile was transferring him to Ceylon (today Sri Lanka), he decided to leave Burma secretly without Bliss.

A Cottage by the Sea in Ceylon

In his new home in the city of Colombo, Neruda would have the same income, and the weather would be just as hot and humid, but he was tired of being in the same place for so long, so he was excited to accept his new post.[7] He sailed for his new post with hope for a fresh and happier beginning.

When he arrived in Colombo, Neruda found a small cottage by the sea. He wrote to his stepmother that the new place reminded him of Puerto Saavedra,

From Rangoon, Neruda moved on to Colombo, Ceylon. The surroundings reminded him of the Chilean seaside.

the Chilean seaside town where he spent many happy days during his childhood.[8] His job as Chilean consul in Ceylon was much the same as it had been in Burma. Once again, he felt that he belonged neither with the ruling British diplomats nor the native people of the island. Neruda wrote, "I had only solitude open to me, so that time was the loneliest in my life."[9]

He woke up early each morning and walked on the beach, practiced his swimming, and returned home to eat lunch and work. His only companions were a dog, a tame mongoose named Kiria, and Brampy, a servant boy who never spoke. Neruda spent his time reading the many books in English that were available in Ceylon. He wrote poetry and hoped that a publisher in Spain would soon accept his new book of poems, *Residencia en la Tierra* (*Residence on Earth*).

Changes Along the Way

In February 1930, Neruda learned that the diplomatic service was transferring him once again. This time his new post, on the island of Singapore, would be busier and more exciting. He decided to bring along his servant, Brampy, and also to smuggle Kiria the mongoose on board the ship to Singapore. When they arrived, Neruda found a hotel room and handed over his laundry to be washed. Then he found out that his new post was actually on another island in the Dutch colonial city of Batavia (now Jakarta). The last ship for Batavia was about to sail. Brampy ran off to collect Neruda's wet clothes, and they hurried to back to the harbor.[10]

While Neruda was staying in a hotel in Batavia, Kiria escaped and was never seen again. Brampy disappeared, too. "My solitude became even deeper," Neruda wrote.[11] Soon, he moved into his official government house and took up his new post, a higher-level job with a better salary than he had before.

During the summer of 1930, Neruda met a young Dutch woman named Maria Antonieta Hagenaar Vogelzang. Neruda called her Maruca, his version of her Dutch nickname, Maryka. He wrote, "She was a tall, gentle girl and knew nothing of the world of arts and letters."[12] Vogelzang was thirty years old, and Neruda was twenty-six. Neruda did not speak Dutch, and Maruca did not speak Spanish, but they each knew a little English.

The couple were married on December 6, 1930. Neruda told his family in Chile, not to worry about his

Pablo and Kiria

Pablo Neruda loved animals. He had enjoyed watching them in the forests of his childhood. He visited every city zoo he discovered in his travels. Among his more unusual pets was the mongoose he adopted in Ceylon. A mongoose is about sixteen inches (forty-one centimeters) long with stiff gray-yellow fur, a native of Africa and southern Asia. It has a fierce nature, but it can be tamed. Known for its ability to kill snakes, the mongoose is lightning fast. Neruda's mongoose, Kiria, had only one encounter with a snake. Surprisingly, she ran at top speed in the opposite direction.

being alone in a foreign place. He now had someone to share his life with. They were poor, but happy.[13]

In March 1931, Neruda's salary was cut in half. Chile's economy was suffering from the effects of the worldwide depression that followed the 1929 stock market crash. At the beginning of 1932, Neruda's post as consul of Singapore and Batavia was eliminated. He and his new wife returned to Chile. His five-year period in Asia was over. More than that, he assumed his country's poverty had ended his diplomatic career.

Back to Chile

The young couple spent two months at sea as they traveled south along the coast of Africa, across the Atlantic and around Cape Horn. They landed at the city of Puerto Montt on the southern tip of Chile. A train took them through the rainy autumn weather of April to Temuco and a reunion with Neruda's family. Neruda's father still disapproved of him. The situation between father and son was not helped by the fact that Neruda had returned home to Chile with no job, no money, and a wife who did not speak Spanish to support.

Neruda and his wife spent only a brief time in Temuco before heading to Santiago. They had returned to a country still suffering from economic and political unrest. Chile's capital city was in turmoil. A new leader, President Carlos Dávila, had just come to power following the overthrow of right-wing dictator Carlos Ibáñez. Yet Neruda found some things unchanged in Santiago. His old circle of friends from his student days

CABALLO VERDE PARA LA POESIA

DIRECTOR: PABLO NERUDA

NÚMEROS 1 - 4

Madrid, Octubre 1935 – Enero 1936

Palabras Previas de Pablo Neruda

Nota Preliminar del Profesor J. Lechner

1974

Verlag Detlev Auvermann KG | Kraus Reprint
Glashütten im Taunus | Nendeln-Liechtenstein

Neruda spent much time trying to find a publisher, he did have success publishing his poems in literary journals like *Green Horse*.

welcomed him back to their life of late nights and long conversations. Maruca did not go out with him to local bars and cafes or join in her husband's active social life. His friends helped Neruda get a part-time job in the library of the foreign ministry. His small salary barely allowed him and his wife to live.

Neruda's finances may have been in a bad state, but his fame as a poet continued to grow. He gave a reading of his work in Santiago on May 11, 1932, to a large crowd of devoted fans. He was still seeking a publisher for his book *Residencia en la Tierra*. He had hoped to publish the book outside of Chile because of the terrible state of the country's economy had made publishing it there a struggle.

At last, in February 1933, a special edition of one hundred copies of *Residencia en la Tierra* was published. The large-size luxury edition was too expensive for many people to buy, but the book Neruda had worked on for five years was finally in print. One reviewer noted the deep appeal of Neruda's poetry for his readers: "The voice of Pablo Neruda has influenced a whole generation in Chile and has even sounded out among other people far from America."[14]

A Circle of Friends

Life in Santiago was very expensive. Neither the publication of *Residencia en la Tierra*. nor the part-time job Neruda had secured at the foreign ministry library brought in a lot of money In August 1933, the twenty-nine-year-old Neruda received welcome news. He had

Spanish poet and playwright Federico García Lorca was executed by Nationalist forces just a few years after befriending Neruda.

been appointed to a new job as Chilean consul in Buenos Aires, the capital of neighboring Argentina. Neruda was relieved to have found work outside of Santiago and in the diplomatic corps to boot.

The move to Buenos Aires was very different from Neruda's move to the lonely isolation of Burma. He quickly formed a new circle of friends among the writers of the Argentine capital. One friend who became very important to him was the visiting Spanish poet and playwright Federico García Lorca, in Argentina for the opening of his play *Blood Wedding*. They admired each other's work. García Lorca signed a copy of his book *Gypsy Ballads* and presented it to Neruda: "For my dear Pablo, one of the few great poets I've had the good fortune to love and know."[15]

Chapter 5

NERUDA IN SPAIN

O nly eight months after arriving in Buenos Aires, Neruda was presented with an exciting new opportunity. A diplomatic assignment had opened up overseas, in a location that had long held an allure for the poet: Spain. Neruda welcomed the chance to become Chilean consul stationed in the port city of Barcelona. In May 1934, he and Maruca boarded a ship for a three-week voyage to the Spanish coast. Another passenger accompanied them. Despite the fact that their marriage was troubled, Neruda and his wife were expecting their first child.

"Where the Poetry Is"

Barcelona was a beautiful city, but Neruda soon found himself longing to be closer to the heart of Spanish literary activity. A friend had told him, "Pablo, you should go live in Madrid. That's where the poetry is."[1]

Neruda decided to take his friend's advice, and prepared to visit Madrid, Spain's capital, in June 1934.

Federico García Lorca, who Neruda had come to know while in Argentina, was now back home in Spain. García Lorca welcomed Neruda at the Madrid train station. Neruda soon found himself at the center of an exciting circle of writers who knew and admired his work. "Within a few days," he wrote, "I was one with the Spanish poets. . . . The Spaniards of my generation were more brotherly, closer-knit and better-spirited than their counterparts in Latin America."[2]

In Madrid, García Lorca belonged to the traveling student theatrical group La Barraca.

Maruca soon followed him to Madrid. They settled into a home they called the *Casa de las Flores* (House of Flowers), made by combining two small apartments. Their home was always open to friends who wanted to join him for drink, food, or literary conversation any time of the day or night.[3] García Lorca was a frequent visitor. He and Neruda were always together. Neruda often visited García Lorca's theater rehearsals. Neruda wrote that García Lorca "was the most loved, the most cherished, of all Spanish poets, and he was the closest to being a child, because of his marvelous happy temperament."[4]

On December 6, 1934, at a lecture at the University of Madrid, García Lorca introduced Neruda as one of the greatest of all Latin American poets. García Lorca told listeners that Neruda's poetry was "closer to blood than to ink."[5] He admired Neruda's power to reach the heart of human emotion and move closer to life than words "ink" would normally allow. In the spring of 1935, Neruda wrote a poem praising his friend, "Oda a Federico García Lorca."

While he worked, wrote, and celebrated life with his friends, Neruda had a heavy weight on his heart. In August 1934, his wife had given birth to their daughter, Malva Marina. The baby had been born seriously ill. Her survival was in doubt during her early months. Neruda watched helplessly as his daughter failed to grow and develop normally. After her first year and a half, she was diagnosed with a condition called hydrocephaly, an enlarged head caused by fluid around the brain. Doctors at that time had no treatment for the condition. Neruda and his wife continued to hope that their child's health would improve.

Conflict on the Horizon

Each afternoon, Neruda and his friends gathered to discuss their plans for the evening. The talk often centered on Spain's political troubles. When he first arrived in Madrid, Neruda said he knew nothing about politics."[6] Even though he worked in the government service, Neruda simply did his job as consul—paperwork and communication. His real work was his writing. Until his years in Spain, he had stood back from the political conflicts that were now becoming more and more threatening.

Spain in 1935 was on the brink of a civil war. The worldwide depression caused terrible economic suffering for the poorest citizens. They looked to the government for some action to improve their lives. Throughout its history, Spain had been a monarchy, ruled by kings and queens. Pressure for change and greater social justice led to the end of the monarchy. Spain then established a republic, a form of democratic government.

The resignation of Spain's King Alfonso XIII divided the country into different camps. Some wanted the return of the monarchy and an end to government reforms. Some wanted greater reforms and a more democratic government. Still others wanted no central government and to turn factories over to the workers. Neruda's friends sided with the Popular Front, the supporters of the new republican form of government. Madrid was the center for support of the Popular Front. The possibility of a violent clash between the various forces grew as the months passed.

At that time, Gabriela Mistral, the famous poet Neruda had met when he was a schoolboy in Tecumo, served as consul in Madrid. When Mistral took a consul position in Lisbon, Neruda opted to stay in Madrid and take her place as Chilean consul. Neruda's wife and daughter went back to Barcelona on Spain's eastern coast, where they would be safer from the dangers of political

Members of the Popular Front march through the streets of Madrid following the municipal elections.

unrest. The possibility of a violent clash between the various forces had grown as the months passed.

Neruda tried to stay busy with his writing, as well as Spanish translations of the works of English poet William Blake (1757–1827). He also continued to meet with friends. One friend Neruda saw often in Madrid was Delia del Carril, a painter from Argentina who had lived in Paris for many years. Del Carril was a beautiful, bright, and political woman; during her years in Paris, del Carril had become a devoted Communist. Nicknamed "La Hormiguita" (Little Ant) for her bustling energy, she was twenty years older than Neruda. He came to admire and love her.

Neruda and the Spanish Civil War

A terrible struggle was about to engulf the Spanish people, especially the poor. On July 17, 1936, carefully timed military revolts broke out throughout Spain and the Spanish colony of Morocco. General Francisco Franco became leader of the forces fighting against the Popular Front republican government for control of Spain. The conflict, called the Spanish Civil War, began that summer and would last for the next three years.

Prior to the start of the war, Neruda's good friend Federico García Lorca had been forced from his home in Granada when he became a target of forces loyal to Franco. García Lorca was being persecuted for his political beliefs and associations, as well as suspicions that he was gay.[7] In August of 1936, he was captured and executed by Franco's Nationalist rebels.

Picking Sides in Spain

The world was watching in 1936 when Spanish army units rebelled against the government of Spain. Countries outside Spain soon became involved. Nazi Germany and Fascist Italy bombed Spanish cities on behalf of the rebel forces of General Franco. The Soviet Union sent supplies to support the Spanish government. In the United States and more than fifty other countries, people joined international brigades to help defend the Spanish government. More than fifty-nine thousand people volunteered to fight. They believed it was a fight for freedom. Famous Americans, including the writer Ernest Hemingway, went to Spain during the civil war. Thousands of foreign volunteers were killed during the conflict. Franco's forces won in March 1939.

The news of García Lorca's death affected Neruda deeply. "And so the Spanish war, which changed my poetry, began for me with a poet's disappearance," he wrote.[8] Neruda knew he could no longer stand back and merely watch as events unfolded. With the death of his friend, Neruda committed himself to the cause of social and political justice, announcing his support of the Republican cause. In the future, he would use his poetry not only to express personal feelings, but to speak out against suffering and injustice. His poetry book *España en el Corazón* (*Spain in the Heart*), which he began writing at this time, would become his tribute to the victims of the Spanish Civil War.

With the first public reading of a poem called "Song of the Mothers of Dead Militiamen," Neruda revealed his new political stand. As a diplomat, he was expected not to take sides in the Spanish Civil War. By speaking openly about his political beliefs, he put himself in danger of losing his job—and also of meeting the same fate as García Lorca.

Support From a Safe Distance

By November 1936, the forces of General Franco were threatening the capital city. It was time to leave Madrid. Neruda traveled with several of his companions to Barcelona. There, he, Maruca, and Malva Marina boarded a train to safety in France. Neruda found a residence for his wife and child near a medical clinic in the seaside resort of Monte Carlo. He traveled on to Paris by himself.

In Paris, Neruda joined a group of writers and kept busy with projects in support of the Spanish Republic. In January 1937, Neruda gave a speech honoring the memory of Federico García Lorca. In his talk, he promised to work for social justice and the welfare of the common working people whose lives were being destroyed by war.[9] Also early in that year, Delia del Carril came to meet him in Paris, and they began a love affair. Del Carril had many friends among the writers and artists of Paris. She introduced Neruda to writers who became his good friends, including the French Communist poets Paul Eluard and Louis Aragon. Chile was officially neutral, not taking sides in the Spanish Civil War. Eventually, however, the government closed its consulate in Madrid, thereby cutting off Neruda's income. "My consular duties had come to an end," he wrote, "because I had taken part in the defense of the Spanish Republic."[10] The loss of his income left Neruda without enough money to support Maruca and Malva Marina. Consequently, Maruca decided to leave France and return to her family home in the Netherlands. Neruda never saw her or their child again.[11]

LIfe With Delia

In Paris, Neruda and del Carril scraped by on the little money he could earn working for the committee for the

General Francisco Franco became the dictator of Spain in 1939, after he staged a coup to oust the Popular Front.

defense of culture. "For months, we ate very little and badly," he wrote.[12] In July 1937, Neruda returned to Spain to attend a writers' congress that he had helped organize. About two-hundred writers from thirty countries came to Madrid to show support for the Spanish Republican cause.

While in Madrid, he returned to his apartment in the Casa de las Flores. He found the roof blown off and the walls damaged by gunfire. All his books and other possessions lay scattered on the floor. He decided to walk away and save nothing from the rubble, not even his books. The scenes of destruction in Madrid seemed too unreal to believe or understand. "War is as whimsical as dreams," he wrote.[13]

Neruda and del Carril left Europe to return to Chile in October 1937. In Santiago, they found a comfortable house to share. It soon became a gathering place where friends were always welcome. In November, the first edition of *España en el Corazón* was published with photos.

When del Carril went home to Argentina to visit her family, Neruda traveled throughout Chile giving public readings of his poetry and raising funds to help victims of the Spanish Civil War. He began thinking of his audience not as a gathering of literary friends, but as the ordinary working people of the world. Filled with a desire to reach out to people and touch their hearts with his poetry, he began to use his poetry as a voice for social justice.[14]

In the late 1930s, the forces of Fascism were rising in Europe, and the Nazi Party gained power in Germany. Chile and other countries had many citizens who were sympathetic to the Nazis. By taking sides against the Spanish Fascist forces, Neruda made himself unpopular with these and other groups in Chile.

In 1938, Neruda faced two personal losses. His father died in May, and in August he lost his beloved stepmother. Neruda went back to his childhood home in Temuco each time to attend the funeral services. Traveling by train, he thought of his father and remembered the train trips of his childhood. His parents and the rainy landscape had formed his life. Memories of his childhood, of his stern, hardworking father and his kind, loving mother would always be part of his poetry.

Neruda to the Rescue

Neruda began using his poetry readings to support the political campaign of Pedro Aguirre Cerda, the presidential candidate of the Popular Front. Chile's Radical Socialist and Communist parties had joined forces in the Popular Front. Neruda's candidate won the election against great odds. Soon Neruda found himself working for Chile's foreign service once again. He was sent back to Paris as special consul for Spanish emigration.

More than half a million Spanish Republicans had escaped over the Pyrenees Mountains to France, fleeing German bombs, Italian soldiers, and the forces of General Franco. The refugees were living in camps under terrible conditions. Neruda's work as special consul was to fill a ship with Spanish refugee families and bring them back to Chile. In April 1939, he and del Carril arrived in Paris and began to organize and carry out the rescue mission. They had many obstacles to overcome. The French government did little to help with the refugee problem, and the government of Chile had little money for the rescue project.

At last, on August 4, 1939, Neruda watched as two thousand Spanish refugees—artists, writers, teachers,

Neruda helped organize the rescue mission that brought thousands of Spanish refugees sailing to Chile on the *Winnipeg*.

farmers, and shepherds—boarded the *Winnipeg*, a ship bound for Chile. Passengers endured hot and crowded conditions during the one-month voyage across the Atlantic. They sailed through the Panama Canal and down the coast of South America to Chile. It was a voyage to freedom and that left Neruda with quite a feeling of accomplishment. He wrote, "There were fishermen, peasants, laborers, intellectuals, a cross section of strength, heroism, and hard work. My poetry in its struggle had succeeded in finding them a country. And I was filled with pride."[15]

Neruda wanted a life of peace, freedom, and plenty for all the people of the world.

The *Winnipeg* docked in Valparaíso, Chile, on September 3, 1939. The Spanish refugees arrived just as World War II began in Europe.

Chapter 6

MIXING POLITICS AND POETRY

Soon after he returned to Chile in January 1940, Neruda settled in a house south of Valparaíso, in the small village of *Isla Negra* (Black Island). The area is not actually an island, but Neruda's home was remote enough to provide almost the same amount of privacy as a secluded isle. The house, Casa de Isla Negra, delighted the nature-loving poet. Tall pine trees grew all around, except where the house overlooked the ocean and the rocky shoreline.[1]

Neruda did not have much time to enjoy this quiet, private place to live and work, however. The government of Chile asked Neruda to serve as consul in Mexico City. Neruda felt it was his duty to share in the political life of his country. At the end of July 1940, Neruda and Delia del Carril sailed north from Valparaíso to the Mexican port of Manzanillo. From there they went to Mexico City.

At Home in Mexico

Neruda and del Carril settled in a large house in Mexico City. Before long, their home became a welcoming place for famous artists and writers of Mexico. Visitors reported that Neruda filled his home with a large collection of seashells and other objects that reminded him of the sea.[2] Neruda was a passionate shopper. He loved the bright colors and fine crafts of Mexico that he found in the outdoor markets. He wrote:

> Mexico is a land of crimson and phosphorescent turquoise shawls. Mexico is a land of earthen bowls and pitchers, and fruit. . . . The most beautiful markets in the world have all this to offer. Fruit and

Neruda enjoyed spending time at his home, Casa de Isla Negra, in the seaside village of Isla Negra, Chile.

wool, clay and weaving looms, give evidence of the incredible skill of the fertile and timeless fingers of the Mexicans.[3]

Refugees from the war in Europe visited Neruda's home, too. He praised Mexico for opening its borders to political refugees. His friend Gabriela Mistral and others helped many people escape from the war in Europe as Neruda had done with the passengers of the *Winnipeg*.

Mexico remained neutral during World War II, but talk of the war could be heard everywhere. Mexico was home to people of a wide range of political beliefs. There were supporters of Communism and also those who supported the Nazi Party in Germany. After the tragedy of the Spanish Civil War, Neruda had strong political feelings himself. As a diplomat for Chile, also a neutral country at the time, he was not supposed to take sides openly. But he could not help expressing his beliefs in his speaking and writing. He sometimes found himself in trouble with the governments of both Mexico and Chile.

When he could escape from his duties as Chilean consul, Neruda worked steadily at his poetry. He had an idea for a long collection of verse called *Canto General* (*General Song*). It would tell the story of the people of Chile. Working in his favorite green ink, Neruda showed each poem he composed to del Carril for her approval. She was a thoughtful critic. Neruda valued her opinion and made any changes she suggested for his work.[4] She spent most of her time entertaining the flood of guests who came to visit, but worked at her painting when she could.

Under Attack

Among the friends Neruda made in Mexico were the great mural painters Diego Rivera, José Clemente Orozco, and David Alfaro Siqueiros. All combined their political beliefs with their artistic work. Like them, Neruda made his personal political beliefs known.

Not long after settling back in Chile, Neruda was called to serve as consul in Mexico City.

He sometimes found himself in conflict with political enemies in Mexico.

In December 1941, Neruda and his friends were attacked in a restaurant by a group of Germans who sympathized with the Nazi Party. Six-year-old Poli Délano, the son of good friends of Neruda, was present on that day. He wrote about the episode years later. He remembered his father pushing him under the restaurant table for safety. Neruda, del Carril, and Poli's parents got into a fight with the party of Germans at the next table. Poli heard glasses breaking and furniture crashing. The battle came to a sudden end when Neruda was struck on the head with a sharp object and began to bleed heavily. "Of course, the Germans disappeared. Tio Pablo (Uncle Pablo) had blood running down his face, and his whole shirt was stained red," Poli wrote.[5] Neruda had to be taken to a nearby hospital, but fortunately his wound was not serious.

Travel, Upheaval, and Tragedy

While living in Mexico City, Neruda also took every chance to travel around Mexico and visited neighboring countries. In Guatemala, he met the novelist Miguel Angel Asturias, who became a good friend. Neruda also visited Panama, Colombia, and Peru. As he traveled, he gained greater knowledge of the wide variety of landscapes and people to be found in Latin America. He took an interest in the lives of the people and the politics of each region.

In 1942, Neruda made his first visit to Cuba. He enjoyed observing life in this Latin American island nation. Neruda and del Carril explored the beaches and forests and found a wonderful new snail shell to collect. They returned to Mexico City with two suitcases full of *polimyta* shells. Neruda could not resist these brightly colored, striped shells of a large Cuban land snail.[6]

In early 1943, the first few poems of *Canto General* were published in Mexico. At that time, Neruda called the work *Canto General de Chile*. In time, the *General Song of Chile* would grow to become the song of all the people of the Americas. New selections of Neruda's poems were also published in Peru and Colombia that year.

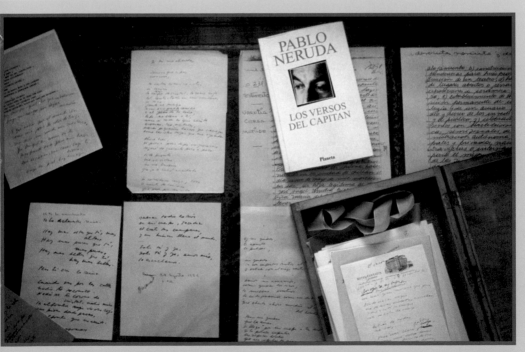

Neruda often wrote in green ink, because he believed the color green nurtured his thoughts.

In March, sad news arrived for Neruda. His daughter, Malva Marina, had died in the Netherlands at age eight.

While the war raged on in Europe, Neruda enjoyed life in Mexico, although his work for the consular service was tedious and dull. It also conflicted with his need to express his beliefs freely. He thought it was his duty as a writer and a human to defend liberty for every person, and that it should be given freely.[7] He asked for a six-month leave of absence and prepared to return to Chile.

Neruda received word that a divorce from his first wife had been granted by the Mexican government. Just before his thirty-ninth birthday, he married del Carril at an outdoor ceremony with songs and poetry. They were a happy and devoted couple despite their twenty-year age difference.

Man of the Americas

During his three-year stay in Mexico, Neruda expanded his knowledge of the history and geography of the Americas. As a poet who loved life, he felt a strong commitment to social and political justice. He wanted to ensure a good life for all people. Neruda wrote that his poetry before *Canto General* was too narrow: "I had probed man's heart; without a thought for mankind."[8]

Through his writing and speaking, Neruda had become a major public figure. Thousands of people attended a farewell tribute for him as he left Mexico. Before returning to Chile, Neruda and his new wife traveled throughout Latin America. They visited Panama, Colombia, and Peru. Neruda wanted to see the ancient Incan city of Machu Picchu in Peru. It was located high in the Andes Mountains. With a guide, they traveled to the ruins on mules.

Neruda's visit to the magnificent stone fortress proved to be a moment of great importance for him. As he later wrote:

> I felt infinitely small in the center of that navel of rocks, the navel of a deserted world, proud, towering high, to which I somehow belonged. . . . I felt Chilean, Peruvian, American. On those difficult heights, among those glorious, scattered ruins, I had found the principles of faith I needed to continue my poetry.[9]

After the visit, he wrote one of his most famous poems, "Alturas de Macchu Picchu" ("The Heights of

Inspiring Ruins

The walled city of Machu Picchu was built by the Incas, Peru's last great Indian civilization. The ruins of the city cling to a steep mountain ridge in the Andes, almost 8,000 feet (2,438 meters) above sea level. The city's huge stones were shaped and fitted together so perfectly that only gravity was needed to keep them in place. The Incas built the city around 1450. The Spaniards conquered the Incas in the 1530s, but they never found the high mountain fortress. An American explorer discovered Machu Picchu in 1911 and told the world. Today more than five hundred thousand tourists a year visit the stone ruins high in the clouds.

Macchu Picchu"). (He spelled the first part of the name with an extra "c.") He explained that his visit to the Incan city helped him see the connection between ancient and modern man. "I thought about ancient American man," he wrote. "I saw his ancient struggles intermeshed with present-day struggles. . . . Now I saw the whole of America from the heights of Macchu Picchu."[10]

Neruda and his new wife visited Uruguay and Argentina before they returned home to Chile in November 1943. In Santiago, Neruda resumed his active social life and also devoted himself to his writing. The need to take part in the political life of his country became greater than ever.

Neruda had long been in sympathy with the Communists who opposed the Fascist forces in Europe. This conflict began with the Spanish Civil War and continued with the Axis powers at war in Europe. In 1944, the Communist Party asked Neruda to be its candidate for senator of the two northern provinces of Chile. These provinces were located in the Atacama Desert, home of Chile's mining industry. Miners in the northern provinces had fought for years for better working conditions and higher wages.

Neruda agreed to campaign by reading his poetry to the people. He was shocked at the poverty and bleakness of life in the desert provinces. "There are few places in the world where life is so harsh and offers so little to live for," he wrote. "I had a childhood filled with rain and snow. The mere act of facing that lunar desert was a turning-point in my life."[11] The memory of what he witnessed at the camps stayed with him for a long time.

Neruda was elected senator for the desert provinces in March 1945. "I shall always cherish with pride the fact that thousands of people from Chile's most inhospitable region, the great mining region of copper and nitrate, gave me their vote. . . . My poetry opened the way for communication," he wrote.[12] In July, he became an official member of Chile's Communist Party.

Writer and Statesman

In May 1945, Neruda became the first poet to receive Chile's National Prize for Literature. He felt deeply the responsibilities he held as a writer and as an elected member of the government of Chile. His voice was not only one of personal expression but of public opinion, too.

Neruda spent the fall of 1945 working on his poetry at his seaside home, Isla Negra. He learned in November that his friend and fellow poet Gabriela Mistral had become the first Latin American to win the Nobel Prize for Literature. At the beginning of 1946, Neruda received the Order of the Aztec Eagle from the government of Mexico. His reputation as a writer and a statesman continued to grow throughout Latin America and the world. Translations of his work appeared in Europe and the United States.

Later that spring, Neruda agreed to serve as campaign organizer for one of Chile's presidential candidates, Gabriel González Videla. The government of Chile was a representative democracy with a president elected from an array of political parties. The Communists and others backed González Videla. He appeared to be the candidate best suited to represent the party's goals. Neruda traveled throughout Chile speaking for González Videla, who won the election by a narrow margin.

Betrayed

Soon after the election, the president began to turn against many who had supported him. After World War II, an undeclared political and economic war began between former allies, the United States and the Soviet Union. Called the Cold War, the rivalry between the two powers spread around the world. In Chile, the United States had great economic interests, particularly in the mines of the north. History and political experts believe González Videla may have turned against his Communist supporters to gain favor with the United States and the anti-Communist forces in Chile. In October 1946, he fired all Communist government ministers. He also agreed to a violent attack on striking coal miners and banned the Communist Party in Chile.

At the end of 1947, Pablo Neruda spoke out against the president he had helped to elect. He first wrote an article for a Venezuela newspaper condemning González Videla's actions. Then he spoke out against him in a speech in Chile's Senate. Neruda wrote, "I am proud of any personal risk suffered in this battle for dignity, culture, and freedom—a struggle all the more imperative for being tied to the future of Chile and to

Neruda's support of González Videla ended once the candidate was elected president and immediately shifted his allegiances.

the unbounded love I feel for the country I have so often sung in my poetry."[13]

González Videla struck back. He revoked Neruda's status as a senator. Without his standing as a senator, Neruda was subject to arrest as a member of the Communist Party. He became a wanted man in his own country. In January 1948, Pablo Neruda went into hiding, on the run from government forces.

Chapter 7

POETRY IN MOTION

Communists across Chile were being thrown in prison in the late 1940s. Neruda had a special target on his back because, in attention to his belonging to the Communist Party, he had publicly challenged President González Videla. As a former senator and a well-respected poet, Neruda would be easily recognized just about anywhere in Chile. Therefore, he decided to go into hiding. An early attempt to move to Argentina without being seen or detected had failed. So Neruda began living a secret life in his native land.

Neruda and Delia moved from location to location, never staying in any one place for more than a week or two. Most of the moves were undertaken at nighttime. The hardship of being on the run was made easier for Neruda thanks to the actions of several friends. At great risk to themselves, these friends offered to have the couple stay at their apartments and country houses. A young man named Alvaro Jara Hantke was in charge of making sure Neruda and Delia made it to each new hiding place safely. The history student was recruited by the Communist Party to perform this secret mission.

At Work in Hiding

During his year in hiding, Neruda continued work on his *Canto General*. He wrote about the land and the people, past and present. Jara Hantke described the sound of Neruda clattering away on his portable typewriter and noted that his life in hiding at least gave Neruda plenty of time to work on his poetry.[1] Neruda wrote during the day, and at night he read his poetry to the friends who were sheltering him. He refused to give up his beloved dinner parties and celebrations, even when he was warned that the noise might reveal his whereabouts.

In 1948, during the Chilean winter months of June and July, Neruda and Delia were hidden with friends in the seacoast city of Valparaíso. Neruda had visited Valparaíso as a student. The city, perched on steep hillsides overlooking the Pacific Ocean, fascinated him. At that time, friends hoped to smuggle Neruda out of Chile on a ship. All the while he kept writing, enjoying the views of the busy streets that he could see from his window. "Trapped as I was in my corner," he wrote, "my curiosity knew no bounds."[2]

The plan to leave Valparaíso by ship did not work out. Neruda celebrated his forty-fourth birthday (July 12, 1948) with a party, conducted in hiding. He wrote with humor about the new suit that his host family had

Neruda signs copies of *Canto General* with painters Diego Rivera and David Alfara Siqueiros, who provided illustrations.

bought him for the failed trip. "I've never had so much fun as I had when I received it," he wrote. "The women of the house took their notions of style from a celebrated film of the day: *Gone With the Wind*."[3] Neruda never lost his sense of humor or his joy of living even in the riskiest and most uncomfortable situations.

By December 1948, Neruda and Delia were once again hiding in Santiago. Their protector, Jara Hantke, agreed to help them organize a Christmas party for all their friends. Everyone gathered at a secret location. No one could leave the party until Neruda and his wife were safely back in hiding. Shortly afterward, during January and February of 1949, Neruda wrote the final verses of his *Canto General*.

Escape From Chile

At last, plans were ready for an attempt to move Neruda out of Chile. An exciting and very dangerous journey was about to begin. Wearing dark glasses and a heavy beard, Neruda began the escape huddled in the backseat of a car. Friends drove him south from Santiago into the forests of southern Chile. On the road, they passed by Neruda's childhood home in Temuco. He later wrote about his feelings as he watched from the car window, "It was my childhood saying goodbye. . . . My poetry was born between the hill and the river, it took its voice from the rain. . . . And now on the road to freedom, I was pausing for a moment near Temuco and could hear the voice of the water that had taught me to sing."[4]

The car headed for a lumber mill in the foothills. From the mill, a group of experienced cowboys would guide Neruda through a rugged mountain pass used by smugglers. Neruda would travel on horseback across the Andes Mountains into Argentina. Neruda had only a few days to practice his horsemanship. He had not been on a horse since his childhood, and the ride would be long and difficult. On March 8, 1949, the group set out. Neruda was carrying a set of false identification papers and a typed copy of *Canto General*. His book was disguised with a false cover and a false title, *Risas y Lagrimas* (*Laughter and Tears*).

The mountain crossing took four days. Twice Neruda's life was in danger, once when his horse struggled to cross a raging river. The horse later slipped on jagged rocks and fell. "I was thrown from my horse and left sprawled out on the rocks more than once. My horse was bleeding from the nose and legs, but we stubbornly continued on our vast, magnificent, grueling way," he wrote.[5] The riders had to hack their way through fallen trees and brush before finally reaching the Argentinean side of the mountain pass and freedom.

Safer in Paris

Once in Argentina, Neruda was driven to the capital city of Buenos Aires. More troubles awaited him. He had escaped the clutches of the police in Chile, but the government of Argentina had been asked to capture him if he managed to cross the border. He had to remain in hiding until he could leave South America. Luckily, Neruda seldom ran short of friends willing to help.

Miguel Angel Asturias, the writer Neruda had met in Guatemala several years before, was now working in Argentina. The two men were good friends. They also looked alike. They had once laughed about their resemblance to turkeys. "Long-nosed, with plenty to spare in the face and body, we shared a resemblance to the succulent bird," Neruda wrote.[6] Asturias offered to let Neruda borrow his passport and his identity in order to leave Argentina and travel to Europe.

Within days, posing as Asturias, Neruda had crossed the River Plate from Argentina to Uruguay and set sail for France. Now that he had escaped the danger in his home country, where would he go? He was famous around the world, not only as a poet, but also as an outspoken member of the Communist Party. Many countries during the Cold War would not welcome a political activist associated with the Communist Party such as Neruda.

Once he arrived in France, he became Pablo Neruda again. Now, he needed the help of friends such as the artist Pablo Picasso, who appealed to the French government to permit Neruda to remain legally in France. "He spoke to the authorities; he called up a good many people," Neruda wrote of Picasso. "I don't know how many marvelous paintings he failed to paint on account of me."[7]

After the 1949 peace conference at which Picasso introduced Neruda as a surprise visitor, Neruda celebrated joyfully with old friends and new. One friend wrote that Neruda was "the man of the hour in the center of the world, hungrily listening and talking, granting ten interviews a day."[8] While in Paris, Neruda met the writer Ilya Ehrenburg, who would soon begin translating Neruda's poetry into Russian. Neruda's work had become an international tool of friendship. In the coming years, while he was still a political fugitive from Chile, his poetry would often make friends for Neruda even among his enemies.

Celebrations and Conferences

In June 1949, Neruda visited the Soviet Union for the first time. He attended the celebration of the 150th anniversary of the birth of the Russian writer Alexander Pushkin, one of Neruda's many literary heroes. Neruda toured Moscow and Leningrad. He enjoyed visiting the scene of the Russian novels he had read as a boy. In July, his wife Delia was able to rejoin Neruda in Poland for his forty-fifth birthday. From Poland, they traveled to Hungary, Romania, and Czechoslovakia. Translations of Neruda's poetry were beginning to appear in these countries and around the world.

In August of that year, Neruda and Delia left Europe and sailed back across the ocean to Latin America for a peace conference in Mexico City. Neruda was happy to return to Mexico and was greeted warmly by friends in the capital city. Neruda's home once again became a busy center for social gatherings. On Chile's Independence Day, September 18, Neruda and his wife

Soviet journalist and poet Ilya Ehrenberg translated Neruda's poems into Russian. He also became a good friend to Neruda.

hosted a celebration. Three hundred guests visited their small apartment, even though Neruda was in bed with a fever, the result of phlebitis, or an inflamed leg vein. He hired a nurse to help out while he was disabled. His nurse, Matilde Urrutia, was from the south of Chile. Neruda had met her three years earlier in Santiago. She was a singer and actress living and working temporarily in Mexico. Neruda and Urrutia formed a close bond that would draw them together in the coming years.

Poet on the Move

In March 1950, Neruda's *Canto General*, the manuscript of poems he had smuggled over the Andes the previous year, was published in Mexico City. Mexican artists Diego Rivera and David Alfaro Siqueiros created illustrations for the book. At the same time, an edition of the book was also being published secretly in Chile from a copy of the poems Neruda had left behind. Also in 1950, the World Peace Council awarded Neruda its International Peace Prize.

After a brief visit to Guatemala, Neruda and Delia set sail for Europe once again. Neruda was still a fugitive, unable to return to his own country. For two more years, he would travel constantly, seeking a safe and peaceful haven. In his travels, Neruda attended peace conferences and writers' conferences and gave readings of his poetry. In January 1951, he visited Italy and read his poetry to large, enthusiastic crowds. The Italian government, however, informed him that he was not welcome. At the very least he would have to avoid making any political statements while in Italy. The French government threatened to deny him residence in France as well.

Neruda and Delia traveled instead to Berlin, Germany. There, Neruda met again with Matilde Urrutia, his former nurse, who had come to Europe to perform with a Chilean musical group. Urrutia wrote later that Neruda gave her a hug and said, "I never want to be away from you again."[9] Neruda began writing a series of love poems for her that would become *Los Versos del Capitán* (*The Captain's Verses*).

In September 1951, Neruda took a train journey with Delia and Ilya Ehrenburg east across the vast expanse of the Soviet Union. Then they flew to Mongolia and traveled on to Peking, China. The following month they were back in Europe, visiting Prague, Czechoslovakia, Austria, and Switzerland.

Neruda and Delia spent the year's end in Italy, visiting Rome, Florence, and Naples, and giving readings of his poetry. In January 1952, the Naples police told Neruda he would have to leave Italy. His permit to stay for three months was canceled. Neruda and Delia left Naples by train for Rome. As the train pulled in to the station in Rome, they saw a large crowd of people waiting. People were shouting, "Pablo, Pablo" and "Let the poet stay!" as the police tried to keep order. Finally, the police prevented a riot by promising the unruly crowd that Neruda would be allowed to stay in Italy.[10]

Later that month, Neruda accepted an offer to stay in a friend's home on the island of Capri off the west coast of Italy. Neruda asked Delia to return to Chile. His new love, Matilde Urrutia, and her small dog came to stay with him on Capri.

Longing for Chile

Neruda spent the last few months of his foreign exile in a peaceful and beautiful setting. He complained to Urrutia that the ocean around their island home did not compare to the coast of his beloved Chile: "If only this sea roared! Its tame waters come to the shore almost silently here; besides, it doesn't smell like our sea."[11] Neruda's book of love poems, *Los Versos del Capitán*, was published anonymously in Naples that summer.

In June 1952, Neruda received the good news that he could return home to Chile. Luckily, his friend Gabriela

Neruda, Hollywood Style

In 1995, Pablo Neruda's stay on the island of Capri came to life on the movie screen. An Italian film called *Il Postino* (*The Postman*) features Neruda as a character. A lonely young man from a poor village gets the job of delivering mail to Pablo Neruda. Neruda receives a flood of mail, much of it from women. The young postman decides that being a poet is the way to find love. He asks Neruda to teach him. Neruda and the postman learn from one another about life and love. *Il Postino* shows in a beautiful way the affection that Neruda and his work inspired in ordinary people everywhere.

Neruda fell in love with Matilde Urrutia while still married to Delia. Their relationship was kept from the public for many years.

Mistral was serving as Chilean consul in Rome. Mistral helped obtain a visa for Urrutia too and also arranged for her dog to travel home with her to Chile. Together Neruda and Urrutia boarded a ship from France for the voyage to South America.

Chapter 8

RETURN TO CHILE

By 1952, although there was still a ban on the Communist Party in Chile, the country's officials were no longer going after individual party members. Without the threat of arrest, Neruda was able to return to his homeland and travel about as he pleased. Upon his return to Santiago on August 12, 1952, Neruda was met by cheering supporters. He wasted no time in speaking out about what he saw as the problems facing Chile as a nation.

He reminded his welcomers that Chile was a rich nation, that produced more copper than any other country. But the people were poor and their children did not have shoes to wear.[1]

At this time, Neruda was living with his wife, Delia, but he continued to spend time with Matilde Urrutia.

Although he loved both women, he knew eventually he would have to choose between them.

Back in the Swing of Things

In his later years, Neruda wrote that his time in Chile from 1952 to 1957 was uneventful, and wonderfully ordinary.[2] In truth, the 1950s was a busy, creative decade for the poet. In the fall of 1952, Neruda used his popular support to campaign for presidential candidate Salvador Allende. Neruda traveled throughout Chile speaking and reading his poetry. It was his chance to get back in touch with his country. He worked hard for Allende's campaign, but Allende was defeated by General Carlos Ibáñez del Campo. Ibáñez kept his campaign promise to lift the ban on the Communist Party. In December 1952, Neruda began a series of yearly trips to the Soviet Union to attend political and literary conferences.

Back in Chile in January 1953, Neruda plunged into work for both his public and his writing life. He organized a conference, the Continental Congress of Culture, to be held in Santiago in May 1953. Writers and artists from all over the world were invited. Neruda spoke to the conference about his goals for equality and social justice for all people. In his speech, he quoted American poet Walt Whitman, one of his literary and political heroes. Neruda explained his feeling that poetry should be available to all. He compared poetry to bread; necessary to everyone: rich, poor, educated, and illiterate. Every person deserved poetry in their life.[3]

Neruda supported defeated presidential candidate Salvador Allende in 1952. Allende finally was elected on his fourth attempt, in 1970.

In December 1953, Neruda was awarded the Stalin Peace Prize (later the Lenin Peace Prize). He used the money from the award to begin building a special house in Santiago. He called it La Chascona, which roughy translated means "wild and tangled," in honor of Matilde Urrutia and her long red hair. The house would be built on a steep hillside close to the city zoo with a view of the Andes Mountains.

In June 1954, Neruda decided to donate his large and valuable collection of books and seashells to the University of Chile. He said of the objects he had gathered with love that it was a collection of items whose beauty had dazzled him.[4] The following month, Neruda celebrated his fiftieth birthday with a gala party at his home at Isla Negra.

Odes to the Ordinary

Also in 1954, Neruda published his *Odas Elementales* (*Elementary Odes*). This was the first of a series of books of odes, or poems of praise. In his odes, Neruda pointed out the wonder of ordinary things. The collection included poems such as "Ode to an Artichoke," "Ode to Salt," and "Ode to a Large Tuna in the Market." *Odas Elementales* was a huge success with readers and critics. Neruda would publish two more collections of odes, *Nuevas Odas Elementales* (*New Elementary Odes*) in 1956 and *Tercer Libro de las Odas* (*Third Book of Odes*) in 1957.[5]

Ties Shaken and Tested

Early in 1955, Neruda asked Delia del Carril for a divorce. The end of his marriage caused a sad break with many of his old friends, who did not approve of his decision. He wrote little poetry for the rest of that year, but he traveled widely and continued his poetry readings. He visited the Soviet Union, China, Eastern Europe, Brazil, Uruguay, and Argentina before returning to Chile early in 1956.

In February of that year, Neruda and Communists around the world were stunned to learn from the Soviet Union about crimes committed by the regime of Joseph Stalin. Neruda wrote, "This revelation, which was staggering, left us in a painful state of mind."[6] Neruda kept his faith in Communism even though he knew about human rights abuses in Communist regimes. He continued to believe that Communism offered the best hope for social justice.

Neruda and Matilde Urrutia spent most of 1957 away from Chile. He began to write *Cien Sonetos de Amor* (*One Hundred Love Sonnets*) for Urrutia that year. Neruda's Communist politics made him unwelcome in many countries during the Cold War era. When he stopped in Argentina to give a series of poetry readings, he was arrested in his hotel on April 11, 1957, and taken to jail. With the help of writers and friends both in Argentina and other countries, Neruda was released a day and a half later. "I was about to leave the prison," Neruda wrote, "when one of the uniformed guards came up to me and put a sheet of paper on my hands. It was a poem he had dedicated to me. . . . I imagine few poets have received a poetic homage from the men assigned to guard them."[7]

Neruda and Urrutia then traveled to Asia. They visited Rangoon and Colombo, where Neruda had served as consul from Chile thirty years before. He found the house where he had lived in Colombo. "I had a hard time finding it," he wrote. "The old place where I had written so many painful poems was going to be torn down soon."[8] Neruda also sought news of his servant, Brampy, and his friend, Josie Bliss. He found no trace of either of them.

From there Neruda and Urrutia flew to China, where they took a trip down the Yangtze River and Neruda celebrated his fifty-third birthday. From China, they traveled on to Moscow and spent several months visiting the Soviet republics of Abkhazia and Armenia. Neruda enjoyed the wonderful new landscapes and cultures. He called the Armenian capital city of Erevan "one of the most beautiful cities I have seen. Built of volcanic tuff, it has the harmony of a pink rose."[9] In October 1957, Neruda and Urrutia visited Finland and Sweden before boarding a ship back to Chile.

Estravagario and *Cien Sonetos de Amor*

During his long year of worldwide travel, Neruda wrote poetry at an amazing pace. The first collection of his complete works was published that year. Back at Isla Negra as 1958 began, Neruda embarked on another presidential campaign tour. Once again he traveled the length and breadth of Chile in support of Salvador Allende, who, although he did not win the election, came much closer than before.

In 1958, Neruda published a new book, *Estravagario*. This collection contained poems that were very personal. He saw himself as complex, puzzling, and full of contradictions—and the poems in this collection attempted to show all those sides. It has been reported that *Estravagario* was among Neruda's favorite books that he had written.[10]

For his dedication to Communism, Neruda was awarded the Stalin Peace Prize, named after Soviet dictator Joseph Stalin.

Animal Attraction

Neruda's gift for humor and wonder helped him find joy in almost every experience. In Erevan, he visited the city zoo. In the zoo's collection of animals was an Andean condor, the national bird of Chile. Neruda recalled trying to make a connection with the raptor, or bird of prey. However, according to the poet himself, "...my countryman did not recognize me. There he stood in a corner of his cage, bald-pated, with the skeptical eyes of a condor without illusions."[11]

Neruda seemed to have better luck with the zoo's tapir. This mammal is related to the horse, but looks like a cross between a large pig and a small elephant. Neruda's connection to the tapir was less where the animal came from, but instead a remarkable resemblance to the poet himself. "[W]ith an ox's body, a long-nosed face, and beady eyes ... I must confess that tapirs look like me."[12]

In early 1959, Neruda and Urrutia visited Venezuela. During a stay of several months, Neruda was named an honorary citizen of the capital city of Caracas. In Caracas, Neruda met Fidel Castro, the leader of a revolutionary government that had just seized power in Cuba. Governments in Latin America looked at events in Cuba with great interest. The United States saw Castro's revolution as a threat to political stability in Latin America.

In December 1959, Neruda published his *Cien Sonetos de Amor* written for Urrutia. He told a writer friend how much she helped him in his life and work.

He found Matilde invaluable. She was patient with his moods and let him live as he pleased so he could write. She helped him stay organized and managed his finances so that he could focus on his poetry. She was his perfect companion.[13]

Urrutia helped the poet both by inspiring him and creating an orderly life at home and on the road.

Natural Disaster

In April 1960, Neruda returned to Moscow once again for the Lenin Peace Prize presentation. He also visited Poland, Bulgaria, Romania, and Czechoslovakia before settling in Paris for the autumn of 1960. There he received the terrible news that a huge earthquake had struck southern Chile. Many towns and cities were heavily damaged. The seaside resort of Puerto Saavedra, where Neruda had spent happy childhood vacations, was destroyed by a tsunami, a giant tidal wave caused by the powerful earthquake.

Neruda returned to Chile in November. He found his new home in Valparaíso seriously damaged by the recent earthquake. Neruda had fallen in love with the seaport city of Valparaíso as a young man fresh out of college and traveling around the country. Before leaving on his travels in the spring of 1960, he had bought a home there. He called the house La Sebastiana after a former owner. It was on a hillside with a view of the ocean. Now the house, full of many of Neruda's books and other treasures, had a collapsed floor.

Neruda and Urrutia traveled the world together. The poet said the woman who would become his third wife created a happy home.

Urrutia wrote that Neruda was especially worried about his big wooden horse from Temuco: "The horse originally came from a hardware store that Pablo passed by every day as he walked to grammar school. He'd always stop to admire it and pet its muzzle. He grew up with the horse and came to consider it somehow his own."[14] Years later, Neruda had been able to buy the Temuco horse and bring it to Valparaíso.

Repairs were made to La Sebastiana. Work was finished in time for Neruda and Urrutia to hold a housewarming there on Chile's Independence Day the following year.

Fruits of His Labors

Books of poetry continued to flow from Pablo Neruda's remarkable imagination. He maintained his schedule of writing every day, most often by hand using his favorite green ink. His work had been translated into languages around the world. Everywhere he traveled, people knew him. In 1961, his Buenos Aires publisher, Losada, printed the one millionth copy of Neruda's most popular book, *Twenty Love Poems and a Song of Despair*.[15]

That year he received an honorary doctorate degree from Yale University in the United States. The following year he began a series of twelve articles about his life for a magazine in Brazil. He would later use the stories as material for his memoirs. In addition to his poetry, Neruda produced many newspaper and magazine articles. He also gave readings and speeches around Chile and throughout the world. He approached his sixtieth birthday as a world-renowned literary and political figure.

Chapter 9

ISLAND OF INSPIRATION

Neruda celebrated his sixtieth birthday by publishing a book named for his seaside estate, where the poems were written. *Memorial de Isla Negra* contained works of memory regarding his childhood and young adulthood. Upon the book's publication, a newspaper reporter asked Neruda if he felt he had achieved his dreams as a writer. Neruda responded that dreaming had nothing to do with his being a poet. Poetry was like breathing or hearing or seeing for him, an essential part of living.[1]

Once again in 1964, Neruda traveled throughout Chile campaigning for Salvador Allende in the presidential election. Allende was defeated yet again. Early the following year, Neruda and Matilde Urrutia took an extended trip to Europe. Neruda's summer travels took him to conferences of writers and peace workers. In June, Neruda received an honorary doctorate degree from Oxford University in England. He was the first Latino to receive this honor. From England, the couple traveled to France, where they spent the month of July, and then moved on to Budapest, Hungary. Finland and Russia were also stops over the course of his travels that year.

Neruda also traveled to Yugoslavia. There he met American playwright Arthur Miller, who invited Neruda to come to the United States the following year for the PEN Club writer's conference. Neruda knew the US government would not welcome a Communist poet. Miller promised to help get permission for Neruda's visit.

New Wife, New Poems

In June 1966, Neruda and Urrutia arrived in New York. Writers from around the world gathered for the thirty-fourth International PEN Congress. Arthur Miller reported that Neruda loved New York and spent many happy hours in the bookshops buying copies of works by Shakespeare and Walt Whitman.[2] Crowds of fans flocked around Neruda while he was in New York. While in the United States, he also visited Washington, DC, to record his poems for the Library of Congress. Then he traveled west to California. Neruda stopped in Mexico and Peru to give readings of his poetry before returning to Chile.

On October 28, 1966, Neruda married Matilde Urrutia. Their wedding took place at Isla Negra with friends looking on. The following month, Neruda published a new collection of poems, *Arte de Pájaros* (*The Art of Birds*). Along with poems about several real birds of Chile, which Neruda knew very well, were works on imaginary birds. For example, "The Shebird" was created for Matilde, while "The Mebird" represented himself. The illustrated *Arte de Pájaros* combined Neruda's love of nature and his great sense of fun.

Neruda's next book, *Una Casa en la Arena* (*A House in the Sand*), also was published in 1966. The title refers to his beloved home at Isla Negra. The collection of poems gave readers a glimpse of the treasures, many relating to the sea and sailing, that filled the house. The names of friends who had died were carved on the wooden ceiling beams. A carved figure from the front of an old sailing ship hung from the ceiling. A ship's anchor rested

Matilde was by Neruda's side by the time he began receiving acclaim for his poetry.

in the sand in front of the house. Mostly, however, the poems in *Una Casa en la Arena* are merely inspired by Isla Negra and his home there. Many are reflections on man and nature.

Still Active

Although his health was failing, Neruda kept up his yearly travel to Europe for peace congresses and writers' conferences. In May 1967, he attended the Congress of Soviet Writers in Moscow, staying in the home of a Russian friend. Upon arrival, one of the first people to address Neruda was an old floor polisher, who wiped his hands before shaking Neruda's, and then recited one of Neruda's poems by heart. This delighted Neruda.[3] The poetry of Neruda had circled the globe. It had found its way into the hearts of ordinary people everywhere.

From Moscow, Neruda and Matilde visited Italy, France, and England. They attended the International Poetry Conference in London. There, Neruda renewed his friendship with Mexican poet Octavio Paz, who later called Neruda "the greatest poet of his generation. By far!"[4] Neruda returned to Chile in August 1967 and resumed his busy writing and speaking schedule.

His next poetry collection, *La Barcarola* (*The Barcarole*) was published in December of that year. Neruda expanded one of the poems from the collection into a play. It told the story of the legendary Mexican bandit Joaquin Murieta. In Neruda's version of the tale, which also delved into the 1849 California Gold Rush,

Octavio Paz eventually became disillusioned by the human rights violations committed by Communist regimes.

Joaquin Murieta is a native of Chile. Neruda enjoyed the experience of writing and producing a work for the stage.

Neruda was in his mid-sixties in 1968 and in poor health, but his creative energy still burned strong. The third edition of his complete poems, published in July 1968 by Losada of Buenos Aires, now filled two volumes. Neruda continued to work at both poetry and politics. At this point, politics, for him, was being involved in the life of the world. It was concern for his fellow man. In an interview for a Mexican newspaper, Neruda said, "You cannot be happy if you do not fight for other people's happiness. . . . Man cannot be a happy island."[5]

By Popular Demand

In September 1969, the Communist Party asked Neruda to put his name in the running for their candidate for President of Chile in the 1970 elections. To his surprise, Neruda won the nomination. The wave of popular support amazed him. "I was in demand everywhere," he wrote. "I was moved by the hundreds and thousands of ordinary men and women who crushed me to them and kissed me and wept. . . . I spoke or read my poems to them all in pouring rain, in the mud on streets and roads, in the south wind that sends shivers through each of us."[6] In the end, Neruda decided to withdraw from the presidential race. He gave his support instead to another candidate he believed in, Salvador Allende.

Political and economic unrest continued in Chile through the months leading up to the September 1970 election. In a surprise victory, Salvador Allende received the most votes. The Congress of Chile approved his election as president in October. Allende became the world's first democratically elected Communist head of state.[7] Allende's leadership was in danger from the beginning. Forces opposed to his policies, including the government of the United States, began working against him. To Neruda, the situation in Chile looked much like that just before the tragic Spanish Civil War began.[8]

Ambassador Neruda

In January 1971, Neruda made a visit to Easter Island, in the South Pacific, 2,300 miles (3,701 kilometers) off the coast of Chile. Neruda visited the mysterious volcanic island as host of a television program on the history and geography of Chile. He would publish a book about his visit in 1972, *La Rosa Separada* (*The Separate Rose*).

While on Easter Island, Neruda learned that he had a new job. He would become Chile's ambassador to Paris.

Chile's Mystery Island

Easter Island is famous for its mysterious stone statues carved hundreds of years ago. More than six hundred huge statues are scattered around the island. Most of the statues are between 11 and 20 feet (3 and 6 meters)high. Some rise as high as 40 feet (12 meters). The early people of the island carved the statues from the rock of an extinct volcano. Scientists are still studying the statues. No one knows yet how the giant figures were moved and set up around the island. Today, Polynesian and Chilean people live on Easter Island. It has been governed by Chile since 1888.

Neruda had asked for the appointment. President Allende agreed that Neruda would be an excellent representative of Chile in the important European capital. Neruda and Matilde set off for Paris in March 1971. One of Neruda's missions was to meet with bankers about Chile's debt to foreign nations. He also planned to seek personal medical advice from doctors in France.

Soon after he arrived in Paris, Neruda underwent surgery. Doctors told Matilde that Neruda had cancer. She decided it was best not to tell him. Neruda celebrated his sixty-seventh birthday in Paris, quietly recovering from his operation. If he knew that he was seriously ill, he showed no sign of it. He continued to work steadily. He planned for the future, including buying a country house in Normandy, on the north coast of France. He later wrote that he wanted a house "where we could breathe with the leaves, the water, the birds, the air."[9]

Receiving the Nobel Prize

On October 21, 1971, Pablo Neruda received the Nobel Prize for Literature. He and Matilde traveled to Stockholm, Sweden, in December for the awards ceremony. His wife later wrote about Neruda's conversation with the king of Sweden. Neruda and the king shared a love of rocks. Neruda described the enormous rocks of Easter Island and invited the king to visit.[10]

Neruda titled his Nobel Prize acceptance speech "Poetry Shall Not Have Sung In Vain." Neruda always referred to poetry as "song" and to writing poetry as "singing." He began his speech with the story of his

Pablo Neruda received the prestigious Nobel Prize in Literature from the king of Sweden in December 1971.

exciting escape over the Andes into Argentina in 1949. Then he spoke about poetry and its meaning and usefulness in human life.

"I have often maintained that the best poet is he who prepares our daily bread. . . . He performs his majestic and humble task of kneading the dough, consigning it to the oven, baking it in golden colors and handing us our daily bread as a duty of fellowship," said Neruda.[11] He spoke of his dream of a new "City of Man" ruled by freedom and justice. In the face of his own illness and political unrest in his country, Pablo Neruda never lost hope for the future of mankind.

Chapter 10

On his writing desk at Casa de Isla Negra, Neruda kept a framed image of the American poet Walt Whitman. Both poets shared an admiration for nature and a passion for social justice. Neruda felt a certain kinship, or family-like tie, to Whitman. In fact, in one work he referred to the American poet as his "essential brother."[1] Of course, Whitman died before Neruda was even born, so perhaps a different relationship was more accurate. When a workman asked if the gray-bearded gentleman in the picture on his desk was the poet's grandfather, Neruda did not hesitate to answer yes.[2]

It was not surprising when, in April 1972, Neruda mentioned Whitman in his address before the United States PEN Club in New York City. He told those in attendance that he owed Whitman an enormous debt:

As for myself, now a man of almost seventy, I was barely fifteen when I discovered Walt Whitman ... the poet who measured the earth with long, slow strides, pausing everywhere to love and to examine, to learn, to teach, and to admire. . . . He is the first absolute poet, and it was his intention not only to sing but to impart his vast vision of the relationships of men and of nations.[3]

Much Beloved

During his visit to New York, Neruda once again visited the shops that sold antiques, seashells, and books. Crowds of admirers flocked around him at all times. He gave poetry readings at the United Nations, the Poetry Center, and Columbia University before returning to Paris. An interviewer asked him how people reacted to his poetry readings. He said, "They love me in a very emotional way. I can't enter or leave some places. . . . That happens everywhere."[4]

Neruda always enjoyed his birthday parties. He celebrated his sixty-eighth birthday at his country home in Normandy, France. He had named the house *La Manquel*, which means "The Condor." For his party, he dressed up in costume as he loved to do. He wore a top hat, a red jacket, and a false moustache. His friends often described Neruda as *un gran nino* (a big child), referring to his playful love of life.[5]

One friend who had sheltered Neruda during his year of hiding in Chile gave thanks for the chance to have lived with the poet. "We are grateful to him . . . for teaching us to value the smallest things: the trees in the park, the stones in the sea, old books, textures, smells, tastes. . . . He had an inexhaustible sense of humor."[6] Neruda's joy in being alive showed in his politics and his poetry.

After a second surgery in Paris in October 1972, Neruda decided it was time to return to Chile. He wanted to go home. After resigning his diplomatic post, he left Paris for the last time in November.

"A Terrorist's Sonnet"

Although it would soon be summer in Chile, the political climate was not warm or welcoming. Economic

With Matilde by his side, Neruda answered questions posed by the press after being awarded the Nobel Prize in Literature.

problems plagued the country. Foreign pressures threatened Allende's government. The United States secretly supported plans to overthrow the Allende regime. US President Richard Nixon and his advisers feared the effects of Allende's socialist policies. Allende took ownership of Chile's copper and nitrate industries away from US companies. Nixon cut off trade between the United States and Chile.

In response, Neruda wrote a short, angry poem, which he called "a terrorist's sonnet," attacking the United States and President Nixon specifically. The work, titled "I Begin By Invoking Walt Whitman," has violent imagery. One stanza, or portion, talks of tearing out " by the roots / this bloodthirsty President Nixon." Another states that no one on earth can be happy "while that nose continues to breathe in Washington." He ends by calling Nixon a "villain who practices genocide from the White House."[7]

A Poetic Light Goes Out

Plans were made for a national celebration of Neruda's seventieth birthday in July of the following year. Neruda decided to offer his own birthday gift to the people of Chile. He hoped to complete eight new books in time for the 1974 anniversary. Seven would be new collections of poems, one for each decade of his life. The eighth book would be his memoirs.

On July 12, 1973, Neruda spent his sixty-ninth birthday quietly with a few friends. He was very weak and remained in bed. One of his visitors was the son of Neruda's publisher. Neruda gave him his seven new book manuscripts. He asked that they be published the following year for his seventieth birthday. He would continue to work on his memoirs for the next two months.

Chilean-American writer Isabel Allende, niece of President Salvador Allende, visited Neruda at Isla Negra that winter. Isabel Allende found the poet unwell. He was frail but still found the vigor to lead her through the labyrinth of his home, filled with his treasures and collections from over the years.[8]

Neruda continued to write. He watched the news on television with increasing sorrow. On September 11, 1973, the military forces of Chile, led by General Augusto Pinochet, overthrew the elected government. The presidential palace was bombed. President Allende died in the fight that followed. Thousands of Chilean civilians were also killed. Neruda wrote the final lines of his memoirs shortly after that day.

Neruda's health declined quickly. Matilde transported him from Isla Negra to a medical clinic in Santiago. He died there on Sunday, September 23, 1973, with his wife and his sister, Laura, by his side.

Matilde decided to have a memorial service for Neruda at La Chascona, their house in Santiago. The house had been ransacked by the military police and was badly damaged. Neruda's wife thought it might help the people of Chile for foreign journalists and diplomats to come to the house and see what the military forces had

Mourners lined the streets of Santiago to pay respects to Neruda. Many took the opportunity to protest the current regime.

done. They had even destroyed the home of a beloved national poet.

On September 25, Neruda's casket was carried through the streets of Santiago to the General Cemetery. The people of the city were forbidden to assemble in large groups. Many risked the danger to follow Neruda's funeral procession. The crowd began to sing and cheer. Armed soldiers watched them with guns ready.

Mystery Solved

Officially, Pablo Neruda died due to complications from cancer. However, a number of people, including his driver, have claimed that forces loyal to General Pinochet were actually to blame. The driver, Manuel Araya, said that Neruda was injected with poison while he was in the Santiago medical clinic.

Rumors of the poisoning, which started after an interview Araya gave in 2011, continued until 2013. To help settle the matter, a judge ordered Neruda's body exhumed, or dug up from its grave. Scientists performed tests to see if any trace of poison could be found. Officials who tested the body's bones found that there was no evidence of chemicals in Neruda's body other than those used to treat his cancer. The theory that the poet was poisoned by political enemies was proved false.[9]

The Work Lives On

Although his final days were filled with sorrow for his country, Neruda's legacy of joy and hope lives on. His vast outpouring of poetry, more than thirty-five hundred pages, has been translated into more than thirty languages around the world. Because Neruda's poetry is available to most of the world's population, one translator calls him "probably the most-read poet in human history."[10] Another translator thanks Neruda "for his generous legacy of beauty and love, his reverence for life, his plea for justice and equality, peace and goodwill."[11] Colombian author Gabriel García Márquez called Neruda "the greatest poet of the twentieth century—in any language."[12]

After the military coup of 1973, it took almost twenty years for democracy to return to Chile. In 1992, Pablo Neruda and Matilde Urrutia, who died in 1985, were buried together in front of the house at Isla Negra. Today

General Augusto Pinochet's military forces overthrew the Allende government, resulting in the president's death.

in Chile, the three homes of Pablo Neruda are cultural centers visited by thousands each year. The Pablo Neruda Foundation at the University of Chile promotes the study and appreciation of his work.

Neruda's fans received an unexpected gift in 2014, when more than twenty unpublished poems written by Neruda were discovered among the poet's personal papers. Boxes of Neruda's work, housed in the offices of the Pablo Neruda Foundation, revealed the amazing discovery. The works were mainly love poems and odes, very similar to other poems Neruda wrote after 1950. The poems were published in Latin America later that year, and in Spain in early 2015.[13]

Preserving the Poet's Memory

After Neruda's death, his wife Matilde took on a special mission. She wanted to preserve his memory by promoting knowledge of the poet and his work. Before her death in 1985, she made plans for the Pablo Neruda Foundation. The foundation restored Neruda's three houses and established a library for scholars. Today the foundation manages the literary legacy of Pablo Neruda. It grants permission to publish his work and uses money earned to support research and writing projects. The foundation gives awards to promising writers. Each year, it honors the best student at the poet's childhood school in Temuco.

Neruda's home in Valparaíso, La Sebastiana, is open to the public as a museum. He and Matilde are buried at Casa de Isla Negra.

Sharing the Passion

Each season of Neruda's life gave him a new direction for his poetry and something new to discover and enjoy. He once told an interviewer, "For me writing is like breathing. I could not live without breathing and I could not live without writing."[14] Neruda's passionate connection to life made the words he wrote "closer to blood than to ink." Readers feel his connection to their lives. His poems ring true in their hearts and stay in their memories.

Around the world, Neruda continues to inspire new generations of readers and scholars who find his voice and his message irresistibly beautiful.

Selected Works

Residence on Earth (1962)
The Heights of Macchu Picchu (1966)
Twenty Poems (1967)
Pablo Neruda: The Early Poems (1969)
A New Decade: Poems, 1958–1967 (1969)
Twenty Love Poems and a Song of Despair (1969)
Selected Poems (1970)
Stones of the Sky (1970)
Neruda and Vallejo: Selected Poems (1971)
Extravagaria (1972)
New Poems, 1968–1970 (1972)
Splendor and Death of Joaquin Murieta (1972)
The Captain's Verses (1972)
Five Decades: A Selection (Poems 1925–1970) (1974)
Fully Empowered: Plenos Poderes (1975)
Memoirs (1976)
Pablo Neruda and Nicanor Parra Face to Face (1977)
Isla Negra: A Notebook (1980)
Passions and Impressions (1982)
Windows That Open Inward: Images of Chile (1984)
A Separate Rose (1985)
Winter Garden (1986)
One Hundred Love Sonnets (1986)
The House at Isla Negra (1988)
The Sea and the Bells (1988)
The Stones of Chile (1987)
Late and Posthumous Poems, 1968–1974 (1989)
Selected Odes of Pablo Neruda (1990)
The Yellow Heart (1990)
The Book of Questions (1991)
Spain in the Heart: Hymn to the Glories of the People at War (1993)
Pablo Neruda: An Anthology of Odes (1994)
Full Woman, Fleshly Apple, Hot Moon: Selected Poems of Pablo
   Neruda (1998)
The Essential Neruda (2004)

Chronology

1904—Ricardo Eliecer Neftalí Reyes Basoalto (Pablo Neruda) is born on July 12 in Parral, Chile. His mother dies of tuberculosis one month later.

1906—His father remarries and moves the family to Temuco.

1910—Neftalí enters Temuco's school for boys.

1919—Thirteen of his poems appear in the Santiago magazine *Corre-Vuelva*.

1920—Takes the name Pablo Neruda; meets Gabriela Mistral who comes to Temuco as high school principal.

1921—Moves to Santiago to study French at the Instituto Pedagogico.

1924—*Veinte Poemas de Amor y una Canción Desesperada* is published.

1927—Receives appointment as Chilean consul in Rangoon, Burma, and leaves for Asia via Spain and France.

1928—Is made Chilean consul in Colombo, Ceylon, and visits India, China, and Japan.

1930—Is made Chilean consul in Batavia, Java, and marries Maria Antonieta Hagenaar Vogelzang.

1932—Returns to Santiago, where there is a severe economic depression.

1933—Appointed Chilean consul in Buenos Aires, Argentina. Limited edition of *Residencia en la Tierra* is published; meets Federico García Lorca, beginning a deep friendship.

1934—Appointed consul in Barcelona, Spain. His daughter, Malva Marina, is born.

1936—Spanish Civil War begins. Federico García Lorca is killed by right-wing forces; Neruda loses his consular post.

1937—Organizes International Writers Congress in Madrid; *España en el Corazón* is published; Neruda returns to Chile.

1939—As Chilean consul in charge of emigration of Spanish refugees, Neruda arranges for safe transportation of two thousand refugees to Chile on the *Winnipeg*.

1940—Appointed Chilean general consul in Mexico.

1943—Divorces from Maria Hagenaar; marries Argentine painter Delia del Carril; resigns his post in Mexico and returns to Chile, stopping first in Peru to visit Machu Picchu.

1945—Elected to the senate of Chile and officially joins the Communist Party.

1947—Defies Chilean President González Videla and denounces him in an open letter.

1948—Is declared an enemy of the government and goes into hiding for a year in Chile.

1949—Escapes over the Andes Mountains to Argentina; travels throughout Europe and visits the Soviet Union.

1950—*Canto General* is published in Mexico.

1952—A new government in Chile revokes Neruda's arrest order; returns to Chile.

1955—Divorces Delia del Carril and moves into a new house in Santiago with Matilde Urrutia.

1964—*Memorial de Isla Negra* is published.

1966—Visits the United States as a guest of the PEN Club in New York; marries Matilde Urrutia on October 28.

1970—Runs for president of Chile but steps aside when Salvador Allende enters the race; after Allende's victory, Neruda is appointed ambassador to France.

1971—Awarded the Nobel Prize for Literature.

1972—Returns to Chile and retires to Isla Negra.

1973—Allende's government is overthrown by the military and Allende dies in the attack on September 11; Pablo Neruda dies in a hospital in Santiago on September 23, 1973.

2013—Neruda's body is exhumed, to look for signs of poisoning.

2014—Previously unseen works by Neruda are discovered.

Chapter Notes

CHAPTER 1. A MAN OF GREAT RESOURCES

1. Adam Feinstein, *Pablo Neruda: A Passion for Life* (New York: Bloomsbury, 2008), p. 237.
2. Donald H. McLachlan, "The Partisans of Peace," *International Affairs (Royal Institute of International Affairs, 1944*), Vol. 27, No. 1 (January 1951), p. 10.
3. Adam Feinstein, *Pablo Neruda: A Passion for Life* (New York: Bloomsbury, 2008), p. 309.
4. Ibid., p. 310.
5. Pablo Neruda, *Memoirs* (New York: Farrar, Straus and Giroux, 1974), p. 140.
6. Volodia Teitelboim, *Neruda: An Intimate Biography* (Austin, TX: University of Texas Press, 2013), p. 311.
7. Manuel Duran and Margery Safir, *Earth Tones: The Poetry of Pablo Neruda* (Bloomington, IN: Indiana University Press, 1986), p. xiii.

CHAPTER 2. NATURE BOY

1. Adam Feinstein, *Pablo Neruda: A Passion for Life* (New York: Bloomsbury, 2008), p. 3.
2. Pablo Neruda, *Memoirs* (New York: Farrar, Straus and Giroux, 1974), p. 10.
3. Ibid., p. 6.
4. Ibid.
5. Feinstein,, p. 12.
6. Volodia Teitelboim, *Neruda: An Intimate Biography* (Austin, TX: University of Texas Press, 2013), p. 20.
7. Ibid., p. 26.
8. Ibid., p. 22.
9. Neruda, p. 12.
10. Feinstein, p. 10.

11. Pablo Neruda, *Passions and Impressions* (New York: Farrar, Straus and Giroux, 2001), p. 242.
12. Teitelboim, p. 28.
13. Neruda, *Memoirs*, p. 16.
14. Ibid., p. 18.
15. Neruda, *Passions and Impressions*, p. 242.
16. Ibid., p. 241.
17. Neruda, *Memoirs*, p. 21.
18. Ibid.
19. Neruda, *Memoirs*, p. 20.
20. Ibid., p. 16.
21. Ibid., pp. 11–12.
22. Feinstein, p. 22.
23. Neruda, *Memoirs*, p. 158.

CHAPTER 3. PROTESTS AND PUBLISHING

1. Pablo Neruda, *Memoirs* (New York: Farrar, Straus and Giroux, 1974), p. 29.
2. Ibid., p. 30.
3. Ibid., p. 32.
4. Ibid.
5. Adam Feinstein, *Pablo Neruda: A Passion for Life* (New York: Bloomsbury, 2008), p. 24.
6. Ibid., p. 30.
7. Neruda, p. 49.
8. Ibid., p. 30.
9. Feinstein, p. 40.
10. Ibid., p. 41.
11. Ibid., p. 43.
12. Neruda, p. 55.
13. Feinstein, p. 45
14. Ibid., p. 64.
15. Ibid., p. 66.

CHAPTER 4. BETWEEN WORLDS

1. Adam Feinstein, *Pablo Neruda: A Passion for Life* (New York: Bloomsbury, 2008), p. 54.

2. Pablo Neruda, *Memoirs* (New York: Farrar, Straus and Giroux, 1974), p. 74.

3. Ibid., p. 86.

4. Ibid.

5. Feinstein, p. 61.

6. Ibid., p. 65.

7. Ibid., p. 64.

8. Ibid., p. 66.

9. Neruda, p. 89.

10. Ibid., p. 102.

11. Ibid., p. 109.

12. Ibid.

13. Feinstein, p. 78.

14. Ibid., p. 92.

15. Ibid., p. 99.

CHAPTER 5. NERUDA IN SPAIN

1. Pablo Neruda, *Memoirs* (New York: Farrar, Straus and Giroux, 1974), p. 116.

2. Ibid.

3. Adam Feinstein, *Pablo Neruda: A Passion for Life* (New York: Bloomsbury, 2008), p. 107.

4. Neruda, p. 124.

5. Volodia Teitelboim, *Neruda: An Intimate Biography* (Austin, TX: University of Texas Press, 2013), p. 179.

6. Feinstein, p. 108.

7. Ashifa Kasam, "Federico García Lorca Was Killed on Official Orders, Say 1960s Police Files." *The Guardian*, April 2015, http://www.theguardian.com/

culture/2015/apr/23/federico-garcia-lorca-spanish-poet-killed-orders-spanish-civil-war.

8. Neruda, p. 122.
9. Feinstein, p. 135.
10. Neruda, p. 126.
11. Feinstein, p. 122.
12. Neruda, p. 130.
13. Ibid., p. 133.
14. Feinstein, p. 132.
15. Neruda, p. 147.

CHAPTER 6. MIXING POLITICS AND POETRY

1. William Karz, "Isla Negra, Chile: An Isle Surrounded by Poetry," Go Nomad, http://www.gonomad.com/21-features/1022-isla-negra-chilc-an-isle-surrounded-by-poetry.
2. Adam Feinstein, *Pablo Neruda: A Passion for Life* (New York: Bloomsbury, 2008), p. 152.
3. Pablo Neruda, *Memoirs* (New York: Farrar, Straus and Giroux, 1974), p. 150.
4. Feinstein, p. 152.
5. Poli Délano, *When I Was a Boy Neruda Called Me Policarpo* (Toronto: Groundwood Books, 2006), pp. 24–25.
6. Feinstein, p. 163.
7. Ibid., p. 167.
8. Neruda, p. 149.
9. Ibid., pp. 165–166.
10. Pablo Neruda, "Heights of Macchu Picchu: XI," *Canto General*, translated by Mark Eisner, *The Essential Neruda: Selected Poems*, edited by Mark Eisner (San Francisco: City Lights Books, 2004), p. 89.
11. Neruda, p. 167.

12. Ibid., p. 166.
13. Pablo Neruda, *Passions and Impressions* (New York: Farrar, Straus and Giroux, 2001), p. 282.

CHAPTER 7. POETRY IN MOTION

1. Adam Feinstein, *Pablo Neruda: A Passion for Life* (New York: Bloomsbury, 2008), p. 205.
2. Pablo Neruda, *Memoirs* (New York: Farrar, Straus and Giroux, 1974), p. 174.
3. Ibid., p. 175.
4. Ibid., p. 177.
5. Ibid., p. 183.
6. Ibid., p. 186.
7. Ibid., p. 187.
8. Volodia Teitelboim, *Neruda: An Intimate Biography* (Austin, TX: University of Texas Press, 2013), p. 312.
9. Matilde Urrutia, *My Life With Pablo Neruda* (Stanford, CA: Stanford General Books, 2004), p. 46.
10. Feinstein, p. 271.
11. Urrutia, p. 104.

CHAPTER 8. RETURN TO CHILE

1. Adam Feinstein, *Pablo Neruda: A Passion for Life* (New York: Bloomsbury, 2008), p. 184.
2. Pablo Neruda, *Memoirs* (New York: Farrar, Straus and Giroux, 1974), p. 224.
3. Feinstein, p. 292.
4. Ibid., p. 295.
5. Rene de Costa, *The Poetry of Pablo Neruda* (Cambridge: Harvard University Press, 1979), p. 159.
6. Neruda, p. 319.
7. Ibid., p. 225.
8. Ibid., p. 229.

9. Ibid., p. 243.
10. Staff, "*Extravagaria* Overview," Barnes and Noble, http://www.barnesandnoble.com/w/estravagario-pablo-neruda/1000410113?ean=9789871138258#productInfoTabs.
11. Neruda, p. 243.
12. Ibid.
13. Feinstein, p. 322.
14. Matilde Urrutia, *My Life With Pablo Neruda* (Stanford, CA: Stanford General Books, 2004), p. 241.
15. Feinstein, p. 330.

CHAPTER 9. ISLAND OF INSPIRATION

1. Adam Feinstein, *Pablo Neruda: A Passion for Life* (New York: Bloomsbury, 2008), p. 337.
2. Ibid., p. 343.
3. Ibid., p. 350.
4. Ibid., p. 353.
5. Ibid., p. 365.
6. Pablo Neruda, *Memoirs* (New York: Farrar, Straus and Giroux, 1974), p. 337.
7. Feinstein, p. 373.
8. Ibid., p. 374.
9. Neruda, p. 339.
10. Matilde Urrutia, *My Life With Pablo Neruda* (Stanford, CA: Stanford General Books, 2004), p. 278.
11. Pablo Neruda, *Passions and Impressions* (New York: Farrar, Straus and Giroux, 2001), p. 386.

CHAPTER 10. WANING YEARS

1. Pablo Neruda, "I Begin By Invoking Walt Whitman," http://hushpoint.blogspot.com/2006/09/i-begin-by-invoking-walt-whitman-by.html.

2. Adam Feinstein, *Pablo Neruda: A Passion for Life* (New York: Bloomsbury, 2008), p. 386.

3. Pablo Neruda, *Passions and Impressions* (New York: Farrar, Straus and Giroux, 2001), pp. 376–377.

4. Rita Guibert, "Pablo Neruda," *Latin American Writers at Work: The Paris Review* (New York: Modern Library, 2003), p. 53.

5. Feinstein, p. 319.

6. Ibid., pp. 213–214.

7. Op. cit., Neruda, "I Begin By Invoking Walt Whitman."

8. Feinstein, p. 404.

9. Bill Chappel, "Poet Pablo Neruda Was Not Poisoned, Officials in Chile Say," NPR, November 8, 2013, http://www.npr.org/sections/thetwo-way/2013/11/08/243949324/poet-pablo-neruda-was-not-poisoned-officials-in-chile-say.

10. Alastair Reid, "Introduction," *Pablo Neruda: Selected Poems* (Boston: Houghton Mifflin, 1990).

11. Jack Schmitt, "Translator's Introduction," *Pablo Neruda: Art of Birds* (Austin, TX: University of Texas Press, 1985), p. 12.

12. Edward Hirsch, "Pablo Neruda at 100," July 11, 2004, http://www.washingtonpost.com/wp-dyn/articles/A37885-2004Jul8.html (June 8, 2006).

13. Alison Flood, "Pablo Neruda Poems 'of Extraordinary Quality' Discovered," *The Guardian* June 19, 2014, http://www.theguardian.com/books/2014/jun/19/pablo-neruda-poems-20-unseen.

14. Guibert, p. 52.

Glossary

alias—A made-up name usually used to conceal a person's true identity.

campaign—The competition between rival political candidates or organizations for a specific purpose or office.

Communism—A system of social organization based on the premise that all property, food, and resources should be shared in common and ownership should be given to the community as a whole.

consul—Government official who lives in a foreign city and protects the government's citizens living there.

coup—A seizure of a government through illegal and violent means.

dictator—One who takes absolute control of a country by being cruel and destructive.

diplomat—One who works in a foreign country as a governmental representative of his or her homeland.

emigrate—Moving to a new country or region.

honorary—Given as a sign of respect or to honor one's achievements.

manuscript—Written pages that together form a book, play, or some other type of story.

memoir—A written account of a person's life and experiences.

pedagogical—Relating to pedagogy; the art and science of teaching, education, and instructional methods.

revolution—To overthrow and replace the government.

tsunami—A huge ocean wave that may follow an earthquake, causing plenty of destruction.

Further Reading

Books

Brown, Monica and Julie Paschkis. *Pablo Neruda: Poet of the People*. New York: Henry Holt and Co., 2011.

Nelson, David E. *Chile (Genocide and Persecution)*. Independence, KY: Greenhaven Press, 2014.

Neruda, Pablo (translated by Jack Schmitt). *Canto General*. Oakland, CA: University of California Press, 2011.

Reef, Catherine. *Poetry Came in Search of Me: The Story of Pablo Neruda*. Greensboro, NC: Morgan Reynolds Publishing, 2015.

Websites

The Pablo Neruda Foundation

http://www.fundacionneruda.org/en

The official website for Neruda's foundation.

Pablo Neruda: The Nobel Prize for Literature

nobelprize.org/nobel_prizes/literature/laureates/1971/neruda-bio.html

Neruda's biography on the Nobel Prize's website.

Poets.Org from the Academy of American Poets: Pablo Neruda

www.poets.org/poet.php/prmPID/279

Biography and selected works of Neruda.

Movies

Il Postino. Directed by Michael Radford. 1994.

Index